Advance praise for
Coaching Football Ain't Easy

This book is proof of Carlin Carpenter's amazing life and coaching career.

-Tami Forbes, Associate Professor of Health, Fitness, and Sport Science

Finally, a football book without the X's and O's. This book is funny, warm, and makes you feel good all over.

-Jim "Spike" Berry, Principal and Football Coach

Through a mixture of charm, wit, athletic ability and hard work, Carlin Carpenter has written a delightful narrative and thoroughly engaging glimpse into the world of small college sports.

-Dr. Perry Bush, Professor of History

Published by Workplay Publishing
Bluffton, Ohio 45817
workplaypublishing.com

ISBN 0-9842122-7-2

Cover design by Alison L. King
Layout by André Swartley
Cover photo courtesy of Bluffton University (by Burton Andrews, 2001)

PRINTED IN THE UNITED STATES OF AMERICA

About the Cover

In this photo, referee Bob Anderson, crew chief, had declared third down for our opponent when actually it was fourth. I went on the field to protest and requested that Bob check with the official scorer in the press box to correct his call. When he refused, I laid down and refused to get up until he checked. He stood by his call and admonished me, "If you don't get up, it will cost you 15 yards for unsportsmanlike conduct and ejection from the game." After several attempts to convince him it was fourth down, I reevaluated the situation and got up. In this case, discretion was a better choice than valor. In spite of his error, we were victorious with a game-winning field goal as time expired; BC 23, Thiel 20.

I reported Bob to the conference commissioner and supported by protest with video. Bob had, in fact, given our opponent one extra down, and he was sanctioned by our league for the incorrect call.

A few years later, Bob apologized for his mistake, and I accepted his apology, "If I were held responsible for all the coaching mistakes I have made, I would be pushing a broom in some two-bit saloon for minimum wage, plus tips."

Bob and I remain friends.

Carlin B. Carpenter

COACHING FOOTBALL AIN'T EASY

Carlin B. Carpenter

WORKPLAY PUBLISHING

Dedicated to Sharon, my wife for over 50 years.
We both never fell out of love at the same time.

Table of Contents

Foreword

Linda Suter

Registrar and Associate Professor of English Emeritus at Bluffton University

Carlin asked my husband Bob and me if we would read his manuscript, *Coaching Football Ain't Easy.* He wanted someone who knew Bluffton University well, yet had never played football and was not particularly interested in the game. As Bob came to Bluffton in 1969 to teach chemistry and physics, and I came in 1967 to teach English, we qualified for Carlin's request.

Carlin tells a fascinating story of his 24 seasons as head football coach at Bluffton College. It is a story well-told: it is informative, detailed and, at times, very funny (as only Carlin can be). He was an imaginative, creative, and sometimes daring coach—so right for Bluffton College.

After reading this book, Bob was quick to say, "Carlin's book is not about numbers, it is about people." Which made me think of Bluffton College Vice President and Dean of Student Life, Don Schweingruber's many-times repeated assertion, "It's all about relationships."

Carlin's book is about relationships he built with hundreds and hundreds of his student-athletes in his 24 years at Bluffton College. The individual stories of individual young men indicate how deeply he cared about the well-being of each and how often Carlin's wife Sharon played a vital part in this relationship. The individual stories follow the player far beyond the football field, even beyond the four years of college, and well into the person's life, his career, and his family. Carlin loved his players.

For me, Carlin's narrative was a journey back in time; I knew all those young men either from a college English class or as the Registrar who may have helped them plan their academic programs, cheered with them when they worked hard and selected challenging classes, and assisted them over academic hurdles if they stumbled. Then finally, I was there to see them walk across the stage as their name was read and I passed their diplomas to the President, who in turn handed them over to the students. I knew these individuals. I felt a pride along with Carlin and their parents and their families. It was team effort.

So, readers, enjoy Carlin Carpenter's book; he is an excellent storyteller. Also, you will recognize in Carlin a person with integrity and care who represents the best values of Bluffton University.

Thanks, Carlin. Go Beavers!

Introduction

For the past 30 plus years, I have been employed in some capacity by Bluffton University, formerly Bluffton College. Twenty-four years were spent serving as head football coach, with 23 of those as director of athletics and coach. In addition, I served as an assistant professor in the Department of Health, Physical Education, and Recreation. I also chaired the department for two years. I retired in 2003 and have since served as Professor Emeritus, teaching in the Department of Health, Fitness, and Sport Science.

Throughout all this time, there have been numerous events that enlightened me, made me laugh, were sad or insane, or were nearly beyond comprehension. It was a time of exhilarating highs and crushing lows. The following describes some of these events worth sharing. A few names of those involved have been redacted or changed to protect their privacy, but the events are, to the best of my knowledge, truthful and accurate.

A Rocky Start

Upon graduating from Defiance (OH) College in 1964, Sharon and I moved back to Nelsonville, Ohio, our home town. Sharon was pregnant with our first child, and Kelly was born on July 3, 1964.

I took a job as a counselor with the Ohio Employment Service in Athens, Ohio, and hated every minute of it. Bob Sheskey, head football coach at Nelsonville High School, asked if I would be interested in coaching there. I jumped at the chance; however, the only teaching position available was one in special education, in which I was not certified. As a matter of fact, I was not certified in anything. My degree was a Bachelor of Arts in psychology and biology without any education courses.

Bob exclaimed, "Not a problem. We'll get you a temporary teaching certificate in special education." I was certified and started teaching and coaching at Nelsonville in the fall of 1965. I took a $2,000 reduction in pay; from $6,000 per year at the Employment Service to $4,000 at NHS. I never claimed to be the sharpest tool in the shed.

We won our first game, the only one.

A PhD Sounds Good

Midway through the teaching year at NHS, Dr. James R. Frey, my advisor at Defiance College, telephoned. He wanted to know if I would be interested in interviewing for a graduate assistant's position as a PhD candidate in microbiology at the University of Massachusetts. I had had enough of public school teaching and informed him that I was very interested, but needed details.

The assistantship included tuition and all fees, plus books and a monthly stipend. The best part of the deal—the person at U of Mass to whom I would be responsible, and the one doing the hiring, was Dr. Frey's best friend.

Slam dunk! I got the assistantship.

Dr. Frey passed away on October 2, 1996. He was afflicted with polycystic kidney disease (PKD), a genetic disorder, which eventually resulted in kidney failure. He died as a result of a surgeon's error following a kidney transplant. We were lifelong friends and fishing buddies. We spent countless hours in his bass boat solving the world's problems. I miss him.

Tea, Anyone?

During Christmas break, we loaded a U-Haul, and Sharon, Kelly, and I moved to North Hadley, Massachusetts, a small town outside of Amherst, home of the University of Massachusetts. As one can imagine, the administration at Nelsonville High School was not very happy that I abandoned my position in the middle of the year.

We settled in our rental home, I enrolled in the winter term, and things were going well in the classroom and laboratory. Defiance College had prepared me well for academic success in graduate school and the research assigned to me by my advisor was interesting and challenging. Each PhD candidate had his/her own office equipped with a small laboratory, which included a centrifuge, small autoclave and incubator, as well as other common items (petri dishes, etc.) used to transfer and cultivate bacteria. Wanting to do a good job for my advisor, I spent countless hours in my lab and enjoyed the work.

However, there was a slight problem. Socially, I was totally out of my element. Massachusetts was settled by the English; remember the Boston Tea Party? Each afternoon, all the members of the department would take a tea break, and attendance was mandatory. I always felt uncomfortable during these gatherings and would rather have been studying or working in my lab. Most of the topics discussed were about cultural events, with an emphasis usually on some form of classical music.

The chair of the department was a pompous ass and always led the discussions. He always chastised me for not joining in, but I didn't understand most questions and damn sure didn't know any answers.

"What did you find most compelling about Schnabel's recording of the complete Beethoven sonatas?"

I kind of knew who Beethoven was, but Schnabel? For all I knew, Schnabel could have been a linebacker for the Cleveland Browns. Once I interjected into the tea conversation, "I like to hunt squirrels, rabbits, raccoons, and noodle for catfish." An eerie silence fell over the room. I had exposed my hillbilly roots!

Oh, how I hated those spots of tea, but things were about to change.

Take this Job and Shove it!

It was Monday in late April, 1966, and after a weekend of sunshine, the snow was slowly melting. Coming from Ohio, we weren't used to the type of winters they have in Massachusetts, so the ground was a welcome sight, be it only small patches here and there. I left for the office earlier than usual because I had to make some culture transfers before class. This was the last step in my class research project that would determine 50 percent of the final grade.

When I opened the office door, I couldn't believe my eyes. My incubator was missing and all of my cultures were contaminated, sitting on the lab bench. What the hell was going on? My first thought was that someone had sabotaged my work, but that defied common sense. I headed to my advisor's office. Maybe he had some answers?

Upon arriving at my advisor's office, he was well aware that I was not in a very good mood, but the situation was going to get more intense. I was advised that the department's chair needed an incubator, and with me having the lowest seniority, took mine. That did not sit well. I was about to confront the head of the department of microbiology at the prestigious University of Massachusetts.

For starters, there was no love lost between the chair and me. I treated everyone with respect, regardless of their social or professional position in life. He felt he was entitled to behave in a manner not acceptable by most. The other PhD candidates were fresh out of undergraduate school and were 21 or 22 years old. I was 27, and a four-year Navy veteran, with part of that service time spent as a corpsman in the field with the Marines and with the Shore Patrol, the Navy's military police. I was no stranger to conflict and certainly was not the least bit intimidated by Dr. Big Shot Chair. I was looking forward to this confrontation.

To make a long story short, I told the chair that he could stick the incubator where the sun doesn't shine and ended with, "I quit!" I left his office feeling liberated.

That was the easy part. Now I had to face Sharon.

On the Move (x18)

After quitting, I went home. As expected, Sharon inquired as to why I was not at work. When I told her I quit, all hell broke loose. We had no money, no job, a daughter to provide for, plus we lived what seemed like halfway around the world from home and now we had no future professional plans.

Our next move was to get out of Dodge. Like so many times, our parents came to our rescue. Thanks to their financial support, we were able to rent another U-Haul, load it in an all-nighter, and Sharon, Kelly, and I headed back to Nelsonville. I drove the U-Haul and Sharon and Kelly followed in our Volkswagen Beetle. When we crossed the Ohio border, I broke out in the "Hallelujah" chorus from Handel's *Messiah*.

After relocating to my parents' home, I found a job as head wrestling coach and assistant football coach at Amanda-Clearcreek High School in Amanda, Ohio. I also had to teach general science, biology, and chemistry. We moved to Amanda.

Joe Dean, my former football coach at Defiance College, was an assistant at Ohio University. I was not happy working in high school and wanted to get into the college ranks. There was no way that would be possible without a master's degree, so I contacted Joe to see if they had any openings. They did. I interviewed and was awarded a graduate assistantship starting in the fall of 1968.

We moved from Amanda back to Nelsonville where we found a house to rent owned by a friend of my father. Monthly rent: $45. Sharon went to work at the First National Bank of Nelsonville as a teller to provide us with some extra financial support while I pursued my degree. A few years later, Sharon's father bought the bank.

Upon graduation from OU in 1970, I interviewed at Hanover (IN) College and Defiance College. At Hanover, the president was friends with my mentor at OU, Frank Ellwood. Frank was a former quarterback and team captain at Ohio State University who also served in the United States Air Force and coached at the Air Force Academy. After being discharged from the Air Force, he joined Woody Hayes's staff as the defensive coordinator from 1962 to 1965.

In 1965, Frank moved to Ohio University. He went to OU as an assistant under head coach Bill Hess, another former member of Woody's staff, and later became offensive coordinator. Because of my connection to Frank, I felt confident that I would get the job at Hanover, but Defiance made the first offer, so I took it. My responsibilities at Defiance were faculty teaching duties, head wrestling coach, and assistant football coach. Sharon, Kelly, and I moved to Defiance in the summer of 1970, where we rented a house on campus.

In the summer of 1971, I received a call from Bill Hess offering me a full time position as head freshman coach at Ohio U. I accepted his offer. First-year players were not permitted to participate on the varsity level as per the National Collegiate Athletic Association (NCAA), but the following year this rule was abolished. Now there was no freshman team, so I was reassigned to coach the varsity defensive line.

Sharon, Kelly, and I packed up and moved back to Nelsonville yet again, where we stayed with her parents while I looked for a house in Athens. In a few weeks, we bought a house near campus, one of two we purchased while working at Ohio University. We remained in Athens four years. During our stay there, we were blessed with another beautiful daughter, Jill, born on December 24, 1972.

For the 1975 season, Frank was offered the head coaching position at Marshall University (Huntington, WV) and took me with him as his defensive coordinator, doubling my salary. We moved to Huntington, where we rented a house and later purchased one.

Before our last game of the 1978 season, Frank was fired—as well as all of his assistants. Frank and the athletic director at Marshall didn't see eye-to-eye, and the AD carried a bigger stick. Plus, we had not won any conference championships.

During the season, we always worked on Sunday from 8 a.m. until 10 p.m., so when I returned home at 9 a.m. on Sunday, Sharon knew we all had been relieved of our duties. I tried to console her with, "There are two kinds of coaches, ones who have been fired and ones who are going to be fired."

She didn't find that too consoling. We had a good cry and started to pack.

Starting Over Again

My contract at Marshall ran through January, plus I was eligible for unemployment compensation. This gave us some breathing room—December and January—to find a job with unemployment as a safety net.

Football coaching positions always opened after the regular season, and I learned that Defiance and Bluffton had openings. I had solid connections at Bluffton and Defiance. First, having graduated from Defiance and coached there, I knew the administration. I of course also knew Dr. Frey, my friend and former advisor who had helped me get the graduate assistantship in Massachusetts.

In the Bluffton corner, a friend of mine named Dave Moyer, who had been a graduate assistant in football at Marshall, and had graduated from both Bluffton College and Marshall, was now employed at Bluffton, along with his wife, Elaine.

I contacted both colleges and received an invitation to interview at each. Defiance was first, and I was well prepared. When I had coached there in 1970, Marv Hohenberger was the director of athletics, and now he chaired the search committee. I wasn't sure how receptive he was to my application, since I had left in the summer of my first year to return to Ohio University, leaving Marv scrambling to find a new coach.

Was he serious about me being their head coach or was this just a courtesy interview? After all, I was a graduate of Defiance and had worked there as an assistant football coach on a team that went 8 and 1 and was nationally ranked. (Also, as head wrestling coach, we won the conference title, the National Association of Intercollegiate Athletics [NAIA] District 22 championship, and qualified three wrestlers for the national tournament at Appalachian State University, Boone, North Carolina. At the national tournament, Clint Dix wrestled his way to become Defiance's first All-American wrestler.)

Based on my performance while employed at Defiance, I had a good feeling about my chances of getting the job, but after the interview, I wasn't so sure. Maybe this was just a courtesy interview after all.

Bluffton was next. The only prior contact I had had with Bluffton College was while playing at Defiance, so I didn't really know much about the institution *per se*. I knew it was Mennonite, whatever that meant. The only word I knew close to Mennonite was Kryptonite, and that was the stuff that killed Superman. I was told that Mennonites were Anabaptist, but thought I had heard anti-

Baptist, and wondered, "What did the Baptists do to upset the Mennonites?"

Dr. Earl Lehman, professor of music, and my friend Elaine were two members on the interviewing committee. Late in the interview, Dr. Lehman asked, "If one team prayed prior to the game and one team didn't, which would have a better chance of winning?" Thinking this might be a trick question, I had to come up with an answer that would satisfy those who believed God was interested in winning football games, while considering the other world problems with which He was dealing.

I put on a serious face and answered, "Whichever team has the biggest tackles would probably prevail."

The committee must have liked my answer in that I was notified a few days later I was their new head football coach. Sharon, Kelly, Jill, and I loaded up and moved to the big city of Bluffton.

Prior to moving to Bluffton, Sharon and I had moved fifteen times. Each time we took a new position, we would rent a house and then buy one. On occasion, we bought two houses at the same job site, requiring a move from one to the other.

True to form, we first rented in Bluffton and then purchased homes twice, for a grand total of eighteen moves. Since getting married, we have owned five homes. Our nineteenth move will be to a small underground apartment at Maple Grove Cemetery, and I hope my twentieth move is up. As wholesome a life as Sharon has lived, she is headed straight to Heaven with at least one free draft pick. I hope she picks me!

Return to Bluffton

Either Marv Hohenberger's invitation to interview really was one of courtesy, or the candidate who got the job was better qualified than me. Whatever the case, Defiance turned me down. I put an exclamation point on my displeasure at being rejected by defeating the Yellow Jackets 21 to 8 on our first meeting, October 20, 1979, at Defiance. The headlines in the *Defiance Crescent News* proclaimed, "Defiance Grad Jolts Alma Mater." Although in truth Michael Morris, freshman running back from Lima (OH) Senior High School deserves all the credit. Michael had 40 carries for 222 yards and two touchdowns.

I had attended Defiance College, starting in 1960, following a four-year stint in the United States Navy. My primary reason for attending Defiance had been to play football. As a matter of fact, Defiance wasn't academically accredited and wasn't awarded accreditation until my sophomore year. At the time, I had no idea what accreditation was or what it meant, and really didn't care. I just wanted to play ball.

While there, I also decided to play baseball as well. Having completed two college courses in the Navy, one at the University of William and Mary and the other at the University of Maryland, I was declared ineligible my first year to participate in football and baseball in intercollegiate competition; however, I could practice, which I did.

During my second year in baseball, Defiance played Bluffton College at Bluffton. Bluffton's team was coached by legendary A. C. Burcky while Bob Reising managed Defiance. The game was played on the baseball diamond adjacent to the library.

My first impression of the campus was not favorable. The baseball diamond was substandard and the outfield was home to numerous trees that one had to negotiate in order to make a play. I don't remember all the ground rules, but one was if the ball went between a certain set of oak trees into the woods, it was either a homerun or double, not sure which.

Anyway, on my way to the field from Founders Hall, I got between a groundhog and its hole and the damn thing charged me, or at least that was my impression of his actions. Then during batting practice, while retrieving a ball from the woods, I encountered a snake, not one of my favorite critters. I pitched that day and lost. Upon our departure from campus, I was glad that I only had to make one more trip there to play baseball and two trips to play football.

Unfortunately my experience at Bluffton as a Definace football player was not very pleasant either. We were never victorious. Defiance played Bluffton my junior year for the conference championship. We lost and both tied for the conference title. I still have headaches every time I think about tackling Mike Goings, et.al.

I never dreamed that 15 years after graduating from Defiance I would be employed at Bluffton College, nor that I would learn to love the place.

***

Rent Increase

When I reported to Bluffton to start work, Sharon and the girls remained in Huntington. Sharon was to sell our house and I would look for one here to buy or rent. Sharon sold the house and I found one to rent. The house was owned by Stan and Carolyn Basinger and Mrs. Basinger managed the rental on her own. Shortly after we moved in, I asked permission to paint the interior at my expense. She agreed and I went to work.

Mrs. Basinger always came to the house to collect the rent. I had paid a month's rent in advance and spent the month prior to the next rent payment painting. I painted every room in the house, including the upstairs bedrooms, stairway, and half bath.

I had spent my college summers painting, and did a journeyman's job. So much so, I invited Mrs. Basinger over to inspect my handiwork; plus, I planned to pay her the month's rent a few days early.

She inspected every room in the house and was impressed, "Carlin, this makes a world of difference in the appearance of this interior. It is so clean and bright!"

We sat down at the kitchen table and I offered an ice tea. As I was preparing to write a check for the rent payment, she proclaimed, "This place looks so nice, I have to raise the rent."

Her proclamation caught me totally by surprise. We had no other place to go, so I reluctantly wrote a check for the new, increased rate. I was out the cost of the paint, plus labor, and now on the hook for higher rent. That was the last time I invited Mrs. Basinger over. From then on, I took the rent check to her house.

1979

My first day on the job, I posted a sign: "Those interested in playing football, report to Burcky Gym on Monday, at 5:30 a.m., dressed for a conditioning workout." Come Monday, 54 players reported. My plan was to see how many were truly committed to playing and how much punishment they could withstand. Thus, the 5:30 start time. Besides the early hour, I was going to make life as miserable as possible for those who reported. The workouts were to continue for six weeks, five days per week, an hour and half per session. The conditioning was to include weight lifting, running, wrestling, and any other physical activity I could think of to challenge them. Who would survive? I did not tolerate any player being late or missing a session.

About the third week, Tom Simms missed a workout. Tom was a senior, 6' 3", 233 pound offensive tackle from East Liverpool, Ohio. Tom had never been late or missed a practice and showed great promise as a leader. Later in the day, he reported to my office to inform me as to why he had missed. "Sorry, Coach, but when I woke up today, I didn't feel well."

"Tom, it is easy to attend conditioning when you feel well. I want players who can come when they are sick. How committed are you to the program?"

"I am committed, Coach!"

"Well, Tom, I will see if you are really committed. Meet me in my office at 4 a.m. tomorrow, followed by a workout, and then another with the team, at 5:30. Don't be late, or you are history."

Tom arrived as instructed, early, at 3:45.

I didn't show, nor had I planned to. Tom waited outside my office until I arrived at 5:15, "How does it feel to count on a person and he lets you down? If I can't depend on you, how do I know you won't fold when we need you most?"

Tom got the message. He never missed again, nor was he late. Tom started for the Beavers his senior year, and was one of our best offensive lineman.

At the conclusion of the demanding winter conditioning program, there remained only 23 surviving players, and they were totally committed. The 23 had withstood hell on earth and lived to tell about it. I gave each a T-shirt inscribed with, "1 of 23." I bet most still have it!

When I retired, many of the 23 attended the gathering recognizing my retirement and presented me with an oak rocking chair. On it was attached a gold plate, "1 of 23, Thanks Coach Carpenter, '79 Bluffton College Football Team." I often rock in it and reflect.

Those 23 were the toughest of the tough.

Roy Deserved Better

In the spring of my first year, I was asked to give the awards to the previous year's players. The awards banquet was held in May and all the athletes of all the sponsored sports, plus cheerleaders, were honored. As one can imagine, it was a long banquet, like four-plus hours.

Nancy Young, cheerleader advisor, presented the cheerleading awards. Nancy was the wife of Roy Young, the coach whom I replaced. As she was introduced and made her way to the podium, I felt that this was going to be a difficult time for her. I had been fired before and knew the anguish experienced by Sharon and me.

She started her presentation by admonishing the administration for allowing me to present the awards to last year's players. I was offended and took her comments as a personal insult. When I presented the awards to the football players, I didn't acknowledge her comments.

It wasn't until a few days later that I realized I should have. I was so consumed with protecting my inflated ego that I couldn't comprehend her position. She was absolutely correct; I should not have presented. Coach Young knew his players personally and could have done a much better job of bestowing the awards, along with remarks about each player's contribution to the team.

I often see Nancy, and she always gives me a hug. I admire her for stating her position and wish I had not taken her remarks as personal, because they weren't. Her standpoint at the banquet was commendable.

No Balls

In 1979 we played in Richmond, Indiana, against Earlham College. Earlham was not a particularly strong team, and I had counted them as a Beaver win in my preseason evaluation of our opponents.

Prior to our pre-game warm-up, we always had fifteen minutes of specialty. Specialty involved the kickers, punters, and return personnel. Before the period started, the managers always had the footballs placed at each station where the specialist practiced.

I coached the punters and noticed that there weren't any footballs at my station. Tracy Tryon, our trainer, was near so I told him to tell the managers I needed footballs. Problem! The mangers had forgotten the balls. We were somewhat embarrassed, but grateful that Earlham allowed us to use some of their footballs.

We won and finished the season 3 and 6.

Kick Ass and Take Names

As the athletic director, one of my duties was to evaluate candidates applying for an open coaching position. Of all the responsibilities as the athletic administrator, I detested this responsibility the most. It involved reviewing all the applications, setting campus visit dates, interviewing the candidates, arranging their schedule for other interviews on campus, taking them to lunch, and giving each a campus tour. In most cases, but not all, it didn't take but a few minutes with a candidate to know if he/she was a good fit for Bluffton. This meant I had to spend my day entertaining—for lack of a better word—a person we had no intention in hiring. In some cases, a candidate coming from a considerable distance would arrive the night before. This meant I had to spend double the time with them.

In 1979, we had an opening for a volleyball coach. When a position came open, we normally interviewed three candidates. I had three scheduled to interview, but one cancelled. Each candidate would arrive on campus at 9 a.m. on consecutive days to start the process.

A woman I'll call Sally was the first candidate scheduled to visit, and she arrived late. When she did arrive, she was dressed in bib overalls, with a game-legged, scraggly dog in tow. You got to be kidding me! What was I going do with her and a lame dog for the next six or seven hours?

Most interviews with other members on the selection committee were scheduled to last for thirty minutes. This was my opportunity to have some fun, plus give me some relief. I escorted Sally and ole' fuzz face to each interviewer, went back to my office, and didn't return for an hour and a half. Sally's last interview was with

President Neufeld. I decided not to push my luck, so I waited in his outer office. Ten minutes later she emerged. That had to be the shortest interview in history.

At the end of the day, I thought I should ask her at least one question, "What is your coaching philosophy?" She proudly responded, "Kick ass and take names!"

The next day, candidate Kim Fischer visited and was hired. Kim became the winningest coach in Bluffton College history, and in my opinion, the best of all past coaches, except Kenny Mast. Dr. Fischer was inducted into the Bluffton College Athletic Hall of Fame in 2000.

Failures of Communication

Behavior of an athlete off the playing field is more important than his/her performance on it. It only takes a couple of incidents in which a few players' bad behavior is generalized until all the team members are perceived as undesirable citizens.

My first day on the job, I was briefed by Dave Moyer that the actions of some of our players were not acceptable in our campus community: not going to class, causing a disturbance when they did attend, throwing food in the cafeteria, violating dormitory standards, and a litany of other substandard behavior.

During our first team meeting, I made it clear that this type of behavior was unacceptable. They were to attend class on time, sit in the front row of seats, sit up straight with both feet on floor, dressed as if they were going to church, no hats, and their mouth would open only to ask and answer questions, otherwise they were to keep it shut. Answer questions by simply stating, "Yes, sir," or "Yes, ma'am." Listen to the professor with your eyes and ears.

Every faculty and staff member was to be addressed by Dr., Professor, Mr., Mrs., Miss, or Ms., or however he/she preferred.

Respect for their position was important; thus, we would address them in a formal manner.

As far as the food throwing in the cafeteria, that behavior would not be tolerated and would result in termination from the team, a call to the player's parents, and suspension from Bluffton College.

Of course, I had no authority to dismiss them from school, but they didn't know that.

Once I had outlined the desired behavior standards expected of the team, I needed to develop a rapport with the faculty and staff to assure them that this was not just lip service. I was committed and serious about how the team members represented our program and I was going to set the example. The first thing I demanded, all coaches must wear a coat and tie to work and they must be punctual. In that I only had one assistant, Dave Moyer, this rule was fairly easy to enforce. Dave and I were to address faculty in the same manner the players were to address them.

Dave had graduated from Bluffton, as well as his wife, Elaine, and at the time, both were employed there, so he wasn't too keen on the Dr., etc. business; however, he did comply under protest. Elaine was chair of the department, our immediate supervisor. I did give Dave a reprieve on calling his wife "Mrs."

My next priority was to learn all the names of the faculty and staff on campus so I could address them properly. Easy! Just get a yearbook and put names with faces. How impressive would that be? Only here two days and know everybody's name preceded by title, yes! Unfortunately, there was a slight glitch in this plan. Either I misread Drs. Maurice Kaufmann's and Richard Pannabecker's names as they related to their pictures or there was a misprint in the yearbook. Maurice's name was under Dick's picture and vice versa.

Early the next day, I passed Dick Pannabecker. "Good morning Dr. Kaufmann!" No response. I didn't think much of it; perhaps he didn't hear me. The next several times our paths crossed, same thing. "Hello, Dr. Kaufmann!" Nothing back!

At this point my only thought was that this sanctimonious jerk is starting to aggravate me! I vowed that the next time I spoke to "Maurice" and he didn't return my greeting, I was going to call him on it.

When I challenged Dick as to why he would never return my greetings, he informed me his name was Pannabecker and not Kaufmann. I apologized for calling him by the wrong name, for my less than courteous behavior, and for anything bad I ever thought or said about him (although I didn't specifically reveal that I'd thought him to be a sanctimonious jerk).

I often visited with Maurice and Dick in Shoker Science Center during my tenure at Bluffton. They were brilliant men, outstanding professors in their fields, and were always interesting conversationalists. Following an office visit with either, I always left inspired to become a better teacher. Dr. Pannabecker passed away in 1997. Often, I see Dr. Kaufmann in church or in Bluffton at the Community Market grocery. I still address him as Dr. Kaufmann.

Bus to Daytona

Most of our recruiting was done in Ohio; however, if a player from out-of-state contacted us, we would follow-up. In 1980, a young man from Chicago, whom I'll call James, contacted us and expressed an interest in attending Bluffton. Normally, we would look at film on the recruit followed by arranging for him to visit campus. I requested film and it was sent.

After reviewing the film, we decided James was talented enough to invite for a campus visit. He had good size—6 feet, 205 pounds—and for a running back, appeared to have above-average speed. In 1979, we had won only three games and were badly in need of a good running back. Maybe James was the answer.

Since most of our recruits lived in Ohio, they could make the round trip for a visit in a day; coming from Chicago was going to be a different story. Upon contacting James, I was informed he had no car and the only possible way he could come to Bluffton was via bus. Anybody who would ride a bus from Chicago to Bluffton had to be extremely interested in our program.

Taking this into account, I encouraged him to make the trip and volunteered to pick him up in Lima, Ohio, upon his arrival. James purchased a round trip ticket and informed me of his arrival time—4 p.m. EST.

Just in case the bus arrived early, I was at the Lima bus station around 3:30. The four o'clock bus arrived, late as usual, but no James. Nor was he on the next bus or the one after that. Wondering if he had actually left, I called his home; no answer. I had given him my home phone number (no cell phones then), so I could only hope that he would call upon his arrival. The only thing left was to go home and wait for his call.

Sure enough, around 2 a.m., the phone rang, "I'm here. Can you come and get me?"

"Where is here, Lima?"

"No, Daytona."

"Daytona, Florida? How in the world could you possibly be in Daytona?"

"I don't know, but it was a long ride."

I pressed him to reconsider his location, "Is there a sign or anything near that would indicate you are in Daytona?"

"Yes. I'm looking at the sign on the counter in the bus station."

"What does it say?"

"Daytona."

"Are you sure?"

"Yes."

"Spell it."

"D-a-y-t-o-n."

After one term at Bluffton, James returned to Chicago, via bus. I hope he made it.

***

Viva Arkansas! Viva Mexico!

Early in the 1980 season, an official from the NAIA called and invited the team to play a game in Mexico City, Mexico. As a result of a scheduling conflict, the team that was supposed to go had to cancel, and they needed a replacement. Our open date fell at the same time in which the game was to be played, so we were an obvious choice.

Of course, I confirmed that we would be interested, but had no money to make the trip. I was informed that the Mexican government was footing the bill, and it wouldn't cost us anything. How lucky can one be?

As an international goodwill exchange, we were to play the University of Queretaro Zorros. I have no idea what a Zorro is. Mexico was attempting to introduce football to the country, and this would expose its citizens to the American game. We were informed that we would be playing in a 40,000-seat stadium, and the game would be televised nationally.

Normally, whenever we played a team, it was customary to exchange film to scout each other. Of course, there would be no film exchange with Mexico, but Dave Barnes didn't know that. Dave worked as an intern at Bluffton, part of the requirements for a master's degree in college student personnel at Bowling Green State University, and served as our "film man." Each week he would film our game and exchange the film with our next opponent.

I thought we would have a little fun with Dave. My plan was to convince him that we were going to exchange film with a Zorros coach in Little Rock, Arkansas, at Taco Bell. He took the bait! I contacted Karen Glick-Colquitt in our public information office and had her arrange an interview with Dave about the trip. She went along with my audacious plan.

In order to fully sell my plan to Dave, I recruited the campus pastor, Rev. Jim Mohr, to travel with him. Rev. Mohr was to keep him company and share the driving to Little Rock. Of course, Jim was in on the ruse. Who wouldn't believe a minister?

Dave spent several days mapping out his route to Arkansas. Each time Dave thought he had the fastest route possible, I would suggest an alternate way. After several changes, I accepted his trip plans. Now, there was a problem in locating the Taco Bell in Little Rock. I had Dave call the home office of the restaurant to get detailed directions to the facility. All that was left was to get a cash advance, pack his clothes, plus a lunch, and get a good night's sleep.

On the day of Dave's and Rev. Mohr's departure from the parking lot of Founders, I met them with their transportation. I owned a two-door, 1970 Plymouth that would barely make it to campus from my home which was only two blocks away. Dave was a little apprehensive about the reliability of my vehicle, but I assured him it was in sound mechanical condition. I had placed a 30-gallon trash can in the back seat to be filled with water prior to them crossing the Sierra Desert. Dave wasn't too keen on geography.

All of those on campus who were in on the caper gathered to see them off. I had purchased kazoos, and each well-wisher had one. Dave and Rev. Mohr loaded their belongings into the car, boarded, and as they slowly departed, we blew a lively tune saluting their departure. As they were about to exit the parking lot, we let Dave in on our secret—he wasn't going to Arkansas. "You've been had, Barnsey!"

I gave him a new name, The Arkansas Traveler.

After graduating from BG, Dave did find his way to James Madison University, Harrisonburg, Virginia, where he serves as Director of University Unions.

The fun was over and we had to get ready for our trip to Mexico.

Mexico

As we prepared for the trip to Mexico, I warned the team that this was not like going to Findlay. A lot of things can—and will—go wrong with international travel, so they had better be prepared for unexpected events along the way.

During this point in the program, we traveled in used school buses that we rented from a company in Beaverdam, Ohio, about seven miles from Bluffton. One of my assistants and I would drive to Beaverdam and I would bring the bus back to Bluffton. I didn't have a license to drive a school bus, but as I understood the law, I could drive if no passengers were aboard. Once the team boarded, we had to have a driver authorized to transport passengers. Normally, we would hire one of the drivers from the local high school. The driver we used the most was Lola Leiber. We all enjoyed her company. The bus rented for $35 and Lola was paid $25.

As I predicted, unexpected events started early. On our way to the Toledo Express Airport, the bus broke down outside of Maumee. We had been running on time to make the flight, but now we had a problem. One of our players, Lee Stubbins, a shade tree mechanic, took a look under the hood, but couldn't get the motor to turn over.

Solution! Flag down the next BIG truck. After a few flag-downs that produced only honks and one-finger salutes from passing truckers, finally a United Parcel Service (UPS) truck stopped. I explained our problem, "We need a ride."

He complied and the team piled in the back of his truck with all of our equipment. I rode in the cab. When we arrived at the airport, a porter asked to carry my luggage. I informed him it was in the back. When he opened the back gate, it would be an understatement to say he was surprised to see what he had to carry to the check-in counter. He called for reinforcements.

Up to this point, except for our bus fiasco, things were going as planned, but trouble was ahead. In order for us to pass through customs at the airport in Mexico, each person in the party had to have his birth certificate. I had reiterated this fact over and over to be certain we would not have any problems at customs; however, I didn't check each person's certificate prior to our departure. That was a mistake! One player had his baptismal record instead of his birth certificate, and he was denied entry.

Now what? From past reports, workers in lower government positions were not above taking bribes. I had to take a chance. Bribery is a major criminal act, and if it failed, I would be in real trouble. Bribing a federal agent in the USA was a serious offense and resulted in prison time, but how about in Mexico?

I moved past the agent to a table a few feet away, then took a $10 bill from my wallet and placed it on the table. The agent glanced down at the money, but otherwise said nothing. That was a relief! Now, I knew he could be bribed. The question I asked myself: *How much will it take to clear this player through customs?* I put out another $10. No response. Another $10 came out. The agent was getting more interested and was now staring at the money. Finally, I laid out my last bill, $20, for a total of $50, and opened my wallet to show it was empty. (Luckily the remainder of my money was stashed in the super-secret, zipped compartment of my wallet.) The agent waved us through.

We finally cleared customs and were bused to our quarters on an Army base. The front gate was guarded by soldiers with automatic weapons. This was quite a change from the security at Bluffton.

Earthquake

Often, I had heard our players complain about the dorm conditions at Bluffton. After witnessing the living conditions in Mexico's Army base dorm, they vowed to never again complain about Bluffton's residence halls. The beds were stacked two high and the mattresses paper thin. No hot water, no lids of any kind on the toilets, and the showers would not drain, leaving one standing in water to one's ankles. Plus, every half hour, night and day, a local transit train would pass within a few feet of the building with a thundering roar that rattled the windows.

We had only been in our quarters for a few minutes when something was preventing me from standing. A few players were also thrown off balance and fell to the floor.

"Earthquake! Clear the dorm!" I shouted.

Not having witnessed such an event or the devastation a quake could cause, we cleared the dorm laughing. Fortunately, it was a minor tremor and no property or personal injury occurred. I had never been in an earthquake before, and to this day, I don't know what made me yell, "Earthquake!" The occurrence was noted by the media back home, and caused some consternation for our safety.

Kodak Film and Tacos

On the day prior to our game the team and coaches were scheduled for a tour of the open markets in that part of Mexico. We had had all of our U.S. currency changed to pesos, and received a pamphlet explaining what each denomination in Mexican currency equaled in U.S. dollars.

At the markets, it was common practice to barter. The vendor would start at his price, the buyer would counter, and normally, a middle price would result that was agreeable to both parties.

One of my assistants on the trip was Greg Brooks. When I was an assistant at Ohio University, I had recruited Greg as a quarterback from Alexander High School, Albany, Ohio, and he served as my football graduate assistant when I coached at Marshall University. I brought him to Bluffton as an assistant, and we worked together for twenty-three years. Greg was a trusted, loyal assistant and made a tremendous contribution to the program.

However, Greg provided some lasting entertainment for us when he tried out the bartering system in Mexico. He had a Kodak Brownie camera, and it ran out of film. After a short time, we located a vendor who sold the type of film he needed. The vendor quoted a price and Greg countered. This went on for several minutes, and finally both agreed on a price, and Greg shelled out what seemed to me like a lot of pesos.

Greg was elated! He had just experienced and conquered the technique of bartering; plus, according to him, he practically stole the film based on what he paid for it.

I was happy for him, but out of curiosity, I checked the conversion ratio in my pamphlet to see what he had paid for the film in U.S. dollars: $34.80. Holy Toledo, Maumee, and Perrysburg! His camera only cost six bucks. Greg got all puffed up and stormed back to return the film, only to find the vendor pointing to a sign, "All sales are final."

Brooksy wasn't finished! That night we ate in a small restaurant near the base. No one in the place spoke English, and we did not speak Spanish. We would point at what we wanted and use our fingers to indicate the number of servings desired. Greg pointed to two tacos and a Coke. He held up two fingers on his right hand for the tacos, followed by one finger for the Coke. He gave the same sign with his left hand to accentuate his point, and proudly spoke the only word he knew in Spanish, "Comprende?" You guessed it! He was served six tacos and six Cokes.

For years, we reminded Greg about the bargain he got on Brownie film in Mexico and what he planned to eat for dessert following his six tacos and six Cokes, another taco and Coke?

40,000 Fans?

At 9 a.m. on the morning of the game, we had our pre-game meal of eggs and coffee on the base. Nothing else, just eggs and coffee—no toast, no meat, no cereal, no milk. The cook would crack an egg, drop it in boiling water, stir it around, and dip out the coagulated remains with a strainer. A hog would have turned up his nose at this stuff.

We arrived at the stadium at 11:30 a.m.to prepare for the 1 p.m. game. The players got taped, dressed, and went through their pre-game warm-up. By now it was about 12:45 p.m. The Zorros were nowhere in sight. Perhaps I had made a mistake on the starting time. We were playing in a 40,000-seat stadium and we and the vendors were the only people there; no fans.

The 1 p.m. starting time came and went; 1:30, still no opponent. Two o'clock and no Zorros yet. Now, I'm starting to get concerned! The players were in full gear and starting to turn on me. They questioned my understanding of the starting time, plus they were getting hungry.

There were two vendors sitting in the stands with two large carriers of candy. I called them over and purchased all they had and distributed the sweets among the team in hopes that this would calm them down. It did just the opposite! Now they were hopped up on sugar and were becoming even more restless.

Finally at 3 p.m., the Zorros moseyed into the stadium, as if the game wasn't to start for two more hours. Their coach informed me, "Yes, the game was to start at one, but some of the players wanted to stop and eat prior to the contest, so we did."

There was little trouble estimating the attendance in the 40,000-seat stadium. I counted on one hand the number who came out to see the game. There were more players than fans. I never did see the camera operators who were supposed to film the game for a national audience.

Bluffton College 41, University of Queretaro Zorros 0.

Slapped!

Pain! Oh, the pain! At 3 a.m., I made my way to the bathroom in an attempt to ease the pain in my lower back. Nothing helped! I tried to walk it off. It didn't go away. Back to the bathroom!

Sharon entered. "What's the matter now?"

Barely able, I responded, "I don't know."

Not too happy that she had to climb out of bed at that hour, she wasn't very sympathetic. I started to lose consciousness. In an attempt to revive me, Sharon slapped me in my face as hard as she could. I went out!

The next thing I remembered was an EMS attendant, Larry Kinn, wheeling me through our living room on a gurney. Emergency lights and siren led the way to the hospital.

Dr. Rodabaugh took one look at me and said, "Kidney stone!"

"What the hell is that?" I asked.

He then proceeded to explain the cause of my pain. After a dose of morphine, the pain finally abated.

I spent the next two nights in the hospital. On the second day, I was to be given a bed bath by one of the female attendants. The attendant who had been taking care of me was quite shapely, so I was looking forward to the experience. Unfortunately, the attendant who bathed me was not the one who had been providing my care. This one looked like Hulk Hogan in drag! She nearly gave me whiplash on each turnover.

On the third day, I passed the stone and was released from the hospital, but my jaw remained extremely sore. Just prior to my release, I asked Doc Rodabaugh, "Does a sore jaw always accompany a kidney stone?" It was then that Sharon informed me of the slapping.

Word spread quickly that I had had a heart attack. I spent most of the 1980 season explaining my ordeal, especially its relationship to football. The press of coaching duties and attending all kinds of meetings day after day led to eating on the run—too many hamburgers and fries, and too few fruits and vegetables. No one ever said that they felt sorry for me, not even my own mother.

According to all of my expert sources, passing a kidney stone is as painful as giving birth. If I were a woman, adoption would be in order.

An Early Breakfast

Being married to a football coach, or any coach for that matter, is not a bed of roses. Most of my time was spent recruiting, at practices and games, or off-season conditioning at the expense of my domestic responsibilities and parenting.

Each day of the year started early and ended late, leaving Sharon with most of the responsibility for managing our home. She would cut the grass, cook, clean, wash clothes, iron, many times take the garbage to the curb, plus care for our two daughters, Kelly and Jill. If the car needed service, she took it to the garage.

She seldom complained; however, one particular day she had reached her limit and fussed over some chore I should have done, but didn't. At the time, the only comeback I could think off was,

"You never cook breakfast!"

In reality, I never ate breakfast, but would normally just have a cup of coffee in the office to wash down a couple of cookies. I made it clear that from now on I wanted her to cook breakfast, and gave her some marching orders: "I want two eggs over easy with no sloppy whites, bacon well done, hash browns crispy, toast not too brown, and chilled orange juice; not cold, chilled. No grits, you know I hate grits!"

The next morning, she woke me with an uncharacteristically loud voice, declaring, "Your breakfast is on the table."

"What time is it?"

"Four, get up!"

"Four in the morning?"

"That's right, get up! Your grits are ready!"

That was the last time I requested for Sharon to prepare my breakfast. Any breakfast after that, at least on her part, was strictly voluntary.

Whenever I think of Sharon's love for me, I'm reminded of a line from a Jerry Lee Lewis song, "…many times I have let her down, but she still comes around, to love what is left of me…"

Colonel Sanders Kentucky Fried Chicken and Japan

Over the years, I have made hundreds of home visits. Many times, because of work schedules, parents were unable to accompany their son on the campus visit. Visiting a recruit in his home gave me an opportunity to talk with his parents, which served to further promote our program. On these visits, I always focused my attention on the mother. In most cases, mom was the facilitator as to where her son was going to continue his education. I called her the influencer.

Greg Brooks (he of the film and tacos fame), Dave Moyer, and Mike Richards, a Bluffton grad and teacher at the local high school, were new to my staff, so I decided to take them with me to visit a wide receiver from Dayton, whom I'll call Mark. Prior to our visit, I contacted Mark's parents and informed them I was bringing Kentucky Fried Chicken, and we could visit over a meal of Colonel Sanders's finest.

Mark seemed to be leaning toward Hanover, one of our league members. His main reason for going there seemed to hinge on the fact that Hanover was scheduled to play a game in Paris, France, his sophomore year.

I did not want to lose this one to Hanover! We did not have a game planned for overseas, but there was no time like the present to schedule one. After all, the planning had to start sometime, why not now?

I revealed my plan, "We are organizing a trip to Tokyo, Japan."

Of course, Greg, Dave, and Mike were completely surprised. Mike's mouth dropped open and Dave stifled a cough and choked. His lungs responded with a blast of air which caused him to spit a mouthful of chicken onto the table, part of which landed on the left lapel of my suit.

I tried to defuse the situation, "Dave, you have to slow down on that chicken. I don't know how to perform the Heimlich maneuver, and I guarantee you, if you turn blue, mouth-to-mouth is out of the question."

Although the snafu was embarrassing, I enthusiastically continued endorsing why Mark would be happier at Bluffton, as opposed to Hanover. We left the home thinking we would be playing against him at Hanover.

To my surprise, Mark committed to Bluffton, but he only lasted one year. Mark turned out not to be as good as I, he, or his parents thought he was. I cancelled the trip to Japan.

Social Congress

The 1981 season was a disaster. Things weren't going well and discipline was at an all-time low. When you're winning, it is easy to stay focused, but losing brings out the worst behavior in players and coaches, and I was no exception.

About half way through the season, with our record at 0 and 5, things looked bleak! Our toughest opponents were still ahead, and players were jumping ship like the proverbial rats. We only had two legitimate defensive ends. Since most big plays occur on the perimeter, and the majority of quarterback sacks come from outside, losing one of them would certainly seal our fate.

Then a player I'll call John, the better of the two ends, missed practice. Losing him would have a major impact on our ability to defend the wide side perimeter and rush the passer. John was a good student, a positive player, and was never late or absent for a meeting or practice. Something was amiss.

Immediately following practice, I went to his dorm in hopes of finding him with a good explanation as to why he wasn't on the field. I approached his room and knocked—no answer. I knocked louder—still no answer.

On an impulse, I checked to see if his door was locked. It wasn't. I gently turned the knob and cracked the door. It was evident why John didn't show. He and his girlfriend were both uncovered, sleeping on their backs, naked, in John's single bed. It wasn't a pretty sight! I quietly closed the door and went to dinner.

John was at practice the next day, and I didn't ask why he was absent yesterday. His presence didn't make a difference on the season's outcome: 0 and 9. Ouch!

Things ended well for John, though; he and his girlfriend both graduated, married, and have two children.

I'll Have You Fired!

Dr. Don Schweingruber served as the dean of student affairs during my tenure at Bluffton. He never lost his temper or raised his voice, and always approached each situation in a logical fashion that one had to admire.

At any one time, there were usually at least three of my players on social probation. Some may even still be probation. Invariably, someone would get in trouble every weekend.

Each Monday, with trepidation, I would grudgingly wait for his phone call informing me, "Saturday, two of your players kidnapped the president and are holding him hostage," or something of that nature.

About once a week, I would pay him a courtesy visit. We would chat for a few minutes, and I would go on my way. One particular day, he had stepped out for a minute, but his secretary assured me of his immediate return. I went into his office and had a seat. While waiting, I noticed the opening under his desk was large enough for me to fit in.

Idea! I will hide under his desk, and when he sits down, grab his leg. Yes, a bit childish, but I couldn't resist the opportunity to amuse myself. When I latched onto his leg, he nearly upset his chair, and it took a few minutes for him to gain his composure.

At Don's expense, we shared a boisterous laugh. We had a good visit, and as I was leaving, I thought I would cause a little more chaos. As I exited Don's office, I slammed his door as hard as I could and screamed, "I'm tired of your incompetence. Come tomorrow, you will be looking for a job!" Passing his secretary, I yelled, "I've had enough of you too!"

Her look conveyed, *What is wrong with this idiot?*

I left with Don having to explain my behavior to his secretary.

Don, being the great guy he is, always claimed, "There is some good in everyone." I hope that includes me.

Payback

I credit Dave and Elaine Moyer for recommending me for the coaching job at Bluffton. I was sorry to learn that they were leaving to pursue other opportunities, but was happy that President Neufeld chose me to pay tribute to them at their last commencement. Both had been students here and served on the faculty, but now it was time to move on. I was happy for them, but sad that they were leaving.

When I received the memo from the president requesting that I give a farewell speech, I started preparing my presentation. It would be easy to proclaim all of their accomplishments, and I was determined to make it a memorable occasion. Before graduation, there was over a month for me to prepare my speech.

I interviewed each and did a considerable amount of research on them. I wrote, and rewrote my talk numerous times. I recorded, on audio tape, what I had written, and played it back to evaluate my diction. After several rewrites, I finally was satisfied with what I had composed.

At that time, graduation was held in Founders Hall. Before proceeding to Founders, those in the processional would gather in Marbeck Center's dining hall, and then march to Founders. I purchased a new robe and hood for the occasion. One's position in the processional was determined by the length of service at the college. Being a new employee, I was near the end of the line, with speakers in the front. For the first time, I would be in front. I was really excited, but a bit nervous knowing the gymnasium would be packed; I wanted to do a good job.

As the administration, faculty, and staff assembled, I quietly took a place in front of the line with President Neufeld and other dignitaries. I did not know exactly my position in line, so waited for further instructions from the president. Time was running short and I still had not been assigned a spot. Finally, I asked President Neufeld, "Where do you want me?"

He responded, "Where are you usually?"

"I'm in the back."

"We are about to start, so why aren't you there?"

"Since I am to give Dave's and Elaine's farewell speech, I thought you would want me up front."

With agitation, Elmer replied, "What speech?"

Oh boy! I caught Don stifling a laugh with his other crony conspirators.

With a red face, I eased my way to the back.

Don had sent me a bogus letter from the president—a forgery! Forgery is a felony and he should have been prosecuted, or at least sternly reprimanded for his chicanery.

I thought that was a callous act over an inconsequential leg grabbing.

Twenty years later, I received an invitation to give the commencement speech at Nelsonville-York High School (formerly NHS), my alma mater. Prior to accepting, I validated the request for fear that Don had some way managed to send me another bogus invitation. He hadn't, so I accepted.

Good Wine, Once

In my efforts to recruit players, cooperation with the admission's staff was of utmost importance. If a student-athlete fell a little short academically, I would always present some redeeming quality about the recruit that might override his academic deficiency. Occasionally it worked, but most times it didn't.

An admission's counselor with whom I often dealt was Arman Habegger. He is one of the nicest persons I have ever met and I continue to consider him a friend to this day. But he went by the book. Seldom did I convince him to admit a student who was short academically, but he always offered to assist me in any other endeavor I deemed important for success of the program. One day, I took him up on his offer.

Founders Hall and Burcky Addition needed an upgrade. Both needed paint and pictures. I requested for Arman to help me paint and hang some action shots. He accepted and we started the makeover. Arman was a good painter and had a lot of good ideas concerning how we could spruce things up. After each evening's work session, we would retreat to my house for refreshments, usually a soft drink and sandwich.

I wasn't sure if Arman drank alcohol, but thought I would test to see if he had a dark side. I purchased a bottle of Simonnet-Febvre Chablis, $22, and had it chilled to enjoy as our beverage following an evening of painting. He has a dark side! That was the last expensive wine I purchased for us to share. His dark side was more than I could afford. After that, Mogen David 20/20 Red was in order, $4.95.

Getting in Trouble

In 1980, there were three weak teams besides us in the conference—Taylor, Manchester, and Earlham. If we were to win any games, it had to be against these teams. On paper, we had little chance of defeating Ohio Northern, Anderson, Hanover, Defiance, Wilmington, or Findlay. We had won one game and tied one and badly needed another win.

On our next to last game, we were to play Manchester College, in Indiana. Manchester had not won a single game, so we felt confident of our chances for success. Our last game was to be against Dick Strahm's Findlay Oilers, which was like playing the Green Bay Packers.

Manchester always played well on their field and had rowdy fans. In an attempt to rally as much fan support for us as possible, I sent a letter to the parents of all of our players encouraging them to attend the game. To make their trip plans easier, I included a map to Manchester, Indiana, with the appropriate routes.

When the game started, there were few Beaver fans present, but as the game was nearing its close, more arrived. Unfortunately, they weren't too happy, in that they had made the trip via Manchester to North Manchester. Not ever having been to Manchester College, I thought it was in Manchester, not North Manchester, where it is actually located. I missed the location of the college by over 100 miles. Needless to say, there were some angry parents.

Then again, Columbus missed Asia by several thousand miles, so I didn't feel too badly about my slight navigational error.

We won, 28 to 21, but few Bluffton fans saw the game.

Cowboy Hats for Sale

I have made some bad investments in my life, but this may have been the worst. I decided to do something to promote interest and visibility in our program, plus raise some money. My plan was to purchase 200 cowboy hats at $5 per hat, and sell them for $10, 100% profit.

Problem: I didn't have $1,000 for the initial investment. All I had to do was convince Ms. Betty Laux, manager of the business office, to permit me to order the hats. After their sale, I would reimburse the college.

I went to Betty's office and laid out my plan. She was reluctant, but I assured her that it was a solid business plan and could not fail. In the business world, how many times can one double one's investment?

After much pleading, she finally agreed to front me the money. I purchased 200 hats in the school's color, and had a block "B" stenciled on the front. I sold 18 hats and gave away 5. Fortunately, a friend coached at a high school in West Virginia with a block "B" as their logo, and with the same school colors as BC. I sold him 177 hats at $4 per hat. Total deficit: $112. Shipping costs? Don't ask! I personally paid them.

That was the last time Betty allowed me to make an investment with the college's money.

***

Just Soup, Please

My first full year of serving as director of athletics was 1980; however, being athletic director and head football coach posed some ethical problems. For example, some might view my appointment as a conflict of interest, because I might favor the sport in which I was the head coach.

Being aware of this potential problem, I made certain I didn't discriminate against any of the other programs. I was determined to make sure that each head coach had the necessary resources to be successful. Whenever any requisition from an opposing sport crossed my desk, I signed it. By doing so, no one could accuse me of favoring my sport.

Besides, all of the sports needed new uniforms and equipment. It was long overdue, and as director of athletics, I was going to do my part to upgrade the athletic department. Whatever any sport needed, they got.

In the spring of 1981, Sue Hardwick, President Neufeld's secretary, called to inform me that the president wanted to take me to lunch at the Black Angus in Kalida, Ohio. The Black Angus was an exclusive restaurant with great food and array of beverages, including spirits. He had never invited me to lunch before, so I was honored. Proudly, I informed the department of his invitation. (The football team had gone 2-6-1 the previous fall, so the luncheon invitation had to be my reward for my administrative skills as athletic director.)

We departed at 11:30 a.m. and President Neufeld started the trip by praising my work with the football program and concluded his praise of me with, "However .."

From past experience, I knew that when "however" entered any conversation, the situation was about to turn ugly. And it did! The president started chastising me for my lack of financial oversight of the athletic budget. He reminded me, as director of athletics, my primary responsibility was to be certain that the athletic budget balanced every year. I responded, "We're not over, are we?" That really set him off!

"Are you saying you don't know you are over budget?"

Then he proceeded to inform me that the athletic budget was nearly $5,000 over what was allotted.

Finally, we arrived at the Black Angus, and he was still chewing on me. President Neufeld ordered a full meal. In fear that he would finish his food prior to me, thus giving him more time to work me over while I completed my meal, I ordered a cup of soup. I am usually a slow eater, but I ate that soup in record time. He ate so slowly I thought his food was going to spoil before he got it down; all the time he was chewing his food and chewing on me. President Neufeld gnawed a hole in the backside of my pants so big one could have dropped a watermelon through it.

After more berating during our return to campus, we finally arrived back in Bluffton. What a relief! As I was exiting the car, he concluded, "Have a nice day."

After that, whenever Sue Hardwick called, I always said a silent prayer, *Please God, don't let this be an invitation for lunch!*

Never, ever again was the athletic department over budget.

King Kong

Most of the time our wives had Dave Moyer and me under house arrest. It seemed like every time we went out, trouble found us. Usually Dave was to blame, or at least that is what I would tell Sharon.

Two-a-day practices are a drag and continue for two weeks prior to start of classes. Without fail, after the first week, players would oversleep, causing them to be late for breakfast. Dave came up with a plan to give them a morning jolt: have a gorilla wake them. At the time, it sounded like a good plan.

We went to a prop rental store in Findlay, Ohio, and rented a gorilla suit. It really looked authentic! On our way home, Dave suggested I put on the gorilla head, get in the back seat, and wave at passing cars. I liked the idea, and jumped in the back. In the first couple of cars, the drivers couldn't see me through the glass, so I stuck my head out the window for the next encounter. The surprised driver swerved and nearly went off the road. For safety's sake, we abandoned the idea.

The next morning, I donned the gorilla suit, Dave attached a leash around my neck, and off we went with Dave leading a gorilla to Bren-Dell Hall for reveille. As we were walking to the dorm, an early morning jogger approached. After my best gorilla impersonation and loud growl, she quickly changed direction. Test completed. It looked real!

During two-a-days, players were instructed to leave their doors unlocked; thus, if I needed to check on them, I would have unimpeded entry. We approached the first room. Dave led me in, and I would gently tug on the corner of the victim's sheet or blanket covering him. The victim's eyes would open about half, and then pop open with palpable terror. Once the player realized what was occurring, we would all laugh until tears streamed down our faces. After each wake-up, the player would follow us to the next room.

When we hit the third floor of Bren-Dell, all the previous wake-ups were tagging along to join in the fun. A student I'll call Rodney was our next prey. Rodney was a little squirrely, so I decided to change my wake-up technique. Instead of gently tugging on his bedding, I placed my gorilla face a few inches from his face and gave a few low growls.

He awoke, screamed, punched me in the face, bolted from his bed as if shot from a cannon, flew to the window, kicked out the screen, shot both legs through the opening, but before he could jump, was pulled back inside by Dave and some players.

The window was hinged at the top and swung out, leaving a relatively small opening. Had it been a window that opened vertically, Rodney would have leaped from the third floor before being rescued, and I would still be in prison. That concluded any further gorilla wake-ups.

No one overslept again, at least not that fall.

I Should Have Been Fired

The Beavers bottomed out in 1981 and 1983: 0 and 9 both years. In '82, we won three games. I was scheduled to go on tenure track in '83, but that wasn't my main concern. My family liked to eat, and with only three victories in three years, there was a good chance I wouldn't have a job to support their habit.

When President Neufeld informed me I was to meet with the Administrative Staff, I assumed they were going to talk to me about victories, or lack of. I recognized they had a legitimate concern. The Administrative Staff consisted of a group of individuals who oversaw the operation of the institution. Its members were: Dr. Elmer Neufeld, President; Dr. Donald Pannabecker, Provost and Academic Dean; Dr. Donald Schweingruber, Dean of Student Affairs; Paul King, Director of Development/Public Affairs; and Fred Amstutz, Director of Admissions. All were good men, and I always felt comfortable in their presence at social gatherings, but this was business.

As customary, President Neufeld always opened his meetings with a prayer. I usually just listened, but this time I silently and fervently joined in. After prayer and some small talk, the first shoe hit the floor; they were not happy with the past three years' record, but would give me two more years to right the ship.

Then the second shoe hit, "After each year, we will review your contract." In reality, this meant I had one year to get things in order.

The only redeeming quality of my work was recruiting. When I reported in 1979, and after winter conditioning, there were only twenty-three players left on the team. In 1983, there were seventy. Actually, more than that reported to fall practice; some quit but remained in school. Each one who stayed in school represented a dollar sign to the college, whether he was on the football team or not.

Based on my winning percentage, I had no grounds to challenge their decision and accepted full responsibility for the poor showing of the football program. I promised to do better, and left the meeting knowing I had at least one year to show progress.

I was thankful for my extended employment, and knew I should have been fired. As the athletic director, I even considered firing myself.

Wanted: Good Looking Girls

Giving campus tours to recruits is an important task. Normally, it is the first time that the recruit has seen inside any of our buildings. A good tour has to be long enough to cover all the campus, but it is important not to bore those on tour. Remember, most of the visiting recruits have toured other campuses, so our tour must be one that is more interesting than our opponents'.

Solution: have coeds give tours; thus, adding a little eye candy to hold the recruits' interest. Plus, we paid students a nominal fee to give tours, so the tour guides also benefitted financially from the experience.

Michelle Butcher worked for me as a paid student secretary. She would type the daily practice plans, file, do other needed clerical work, and run errands. Once I decided to use females as tour guides, I asked her to coordinate the program. She was instructed to place signs around campus advertising our need and to screen those interested. In passing, I advised her, "Make sure the girls are good looking."

As instructed, she put up signs inscribed with, "Wanted: Females to Give Football Tours. Must be Good Looking."

The instant the first sign was posted, my phone started ringing and rang for the next two hours. The athletic department phone system lit up like a Christmas tree. Unfortunately, the calls were not from girls wanting to give tours, but those berating me for advertising for good looking candidates. "Why can't ugly girls give tours?" "You are a male chauvinist pig!" were a couple of comments from distraught callers. Some female faculty members even weighed in.

To this day, I don't see why this was so offensive. Ugliness is a relative term. If someone thinks someone else is ugly, he/she probably is. I'm ugly! Abraham Lincoln is the only person uglier than me, but I'm loaded with hillbilly charm. Accentuate your positive qualities and move on.

The signs came down.

Sparky Curtiss

Communication between coaches in the press box and those on the field is very important. Normally, the offensive and defensive coordinators were stationed in the press box and would relay information via head phones to the coaches on the field. Over the years, we have experimented with different types of phones, from wired lines, to remote CB phones, back to wired, and finally wireless.

Our first change was from wired to remote CB phones. The CB phones were programmed with a supposedly secure channel. We soon discovered that the secured channel was anything but secure. Often during the heat of the battle, a trucker travelling interstate 75 would break in on our conversation. Soon after that, we abandoned those and went back to the wired set.

The first time we used the wired set was during a developing thunderstorm. Normally, with any threat of lightning, the game was delayed; however, on this particular day, the lightning seemed far enough away that there was no immediate danger.

Wrong! Lightening hit somewhere in the distance and came through our line and exited out defensive coordinator Allen Curtiss's head set. He suffered a slight burn on both ears, and from then on, we called him Sparky. On Allen's persistence, we changed to wireless, which are still being used today.

After serving fifteen years on my staff and a total of twenty years at Bluffton, Coach Curtiss left in 2008 to be an assistant at Ferris State University (Big Rapids, MI). During Allen's tenure as our defensive coordinator, BC's defense was always ranked at the top or near the top of our conference, year after year.

Spaghetti for Breakfast

Over the years, there have been as many theories concerning the optimum pre-game meal as there are programs. Whenever a team is winning, that is the pre-game *du jour*. I was looking for something that would give us an unfair advantage and theorized that a super-secret pre-game meal might do it.

I contacted our dietitian, Barbara Stettler, and requested her advice. According to Barb, carbohydrate loading is best for supplying energy around five hours after consumption. Barb explained the metabolic aspect of carbs, which I didn't understand. Barb was an expert in food science, but most of what she said went over my head. I always acted like I understood. "So what is the best and cheapest source of food that will provide the most carbohydrates?" I asked.

Barb did not hesitate, "Spaghetti!"

Sounded good to me. Now, I had to convince the players to eat spaghetti for breakfast. After a lengthy meeting with our team, with Barb doing the explaining, I informed the players, "From now on, we are having spaghetti for our pre-game meal."

Our next game was away, which meant we had to eat pre-game at 6 a.m. Not good! Half of the team got sick just seeing spaghetti at that hour. One actually vomited. After staving off a near team exodus, I changed our pre-game meal to bacon and eggs. That made more sense. Nothing that they ate played much of a part in their play. They still had to have talent.

***

M.O.R.E. than Football

The football team is the largest single group on campus. There is no other organization that has more members or has a higher profile. Just by sheer numbers, we could have a positive or negative impact on campus. Whenever a team member violated campus or community standards, his behavior made the news. The headlines always included the fact that the person in question was a football player and never indicated that he was a chemistry major, teacher candidate, or any other academic area with which he was associated.

Most of my time was consumed by dealing with social or academic issues involving players who lacked social skills and values. About 90% of my time was spent on 10% of those violating campus and/or community standards. The catch was I never knew which 10% was going to emerge at any given time.

I contacted Dr. Don Schweingruber, Dean of Student Affairs, seeking a solution to behavioral problems. Since Don was ultimately responsible for dealing with these glitches, he was eager to embrace anything that would reduce his work load, particularly unacceptable behavior by football players.

Don's solution: formulate a program that would address potential behavioral problems before they occurred; thus, the "M.O.R.E than Football" program was founded. M.O.R. E. is an acronym for Motivation, Organization, Responsibility, and Excellence. During preseason practice, we would spend two hours per day, for five days, on subjects that would make the players better citizens. We would also include all the support personnel in the sessions, including coaches.

Topics and presenters were selected and a variety of areas were explored. Some of the topics and speakers were: "The Importance of YOU," Don Schweingruber; "Understanding and Appreciating the Differences in Others," Howard Ward, Vice President for Student Affairs, Ohio Northern University; "On Being a Sexual Being," Kay Parent, health educator and supervisor, Allen County Health Department, along with Linda Fortman, health educator from the same department; plus Linda Kaufman, rape survivor advocate; and "The ONLY Choice, Excellence," William Hawk, Dean of Academic Affairs, Bluffton College.

Other topics covered were, "Where is God in All of This?" by Randy Keeler, Campus Pastor, BC; and "Manners 101," Barbara Stettler and Linda Niehm, Home Economics professors at Bluffton. Jodie Shearer covered "Job Interview Protocol," as a representative from our Career Development Center; and Father Gary Ferguson, priest at Bluffton's St. Mary's Catholic Church, discussed "Those Brain Killing Substances."

We always included someone from Buildings and Grounds. To me, they are the heart of the college—try running an institution without their expertise. Those who were often included were Darrell Huber, Larry Kinn, Roger Luginbuhl, Fred Rodabaugh, and Sarah Woods. They all played an important role in keeping the college running smoothly and were always working on some project in the athletic department to upgrade our facilities. Over the years, I have made so many requests for the B&G crew to repair or build something that they gave me a new name—"Hemorrhoid", claiming I was a pain in their ass, but they never refused any reasonable request.

The final speaker was Gene Slaughter, professor of Sports Management, Capital University (Columbus, OH). Gene's topic, "And Then Some," was the impact each player had on our campus, be it positive or negative.

To showcase our vocal talent, Deb Brubaker, of our music department, wrote a song about the team that we sang as the only football chorale ensemble in the history of the school, maybe in the history of the world. We had some fun!

From M.O.R.E. came the Beaver Code of Conduct, which each player was obligated to follow: do what is right, do your very best, and treat others as you want to be treated. I stole this concept from Coach Lou Holtz, University of Notre Dame.

In addition, every player was required to memorize the Beaver Pledge, which the team recited at the conclusion of all practices and before and after each game. "I believe in God, myself, Bluffton College, team and program; I believe in setting attainable goals and working with the dedication needed to achieve these goals; I believe in the ability to adjust to and overcome adverse situations. I believe!"

M.O.R.E. started in 1990, and in 1993 the regional and national press picked up on the program and gave it national recognition. In 1997, Bluffton College became the first NCAA Division III institution in the United States to implement a program to deal with social and academic issues facing all student-athletes. We called it BChamps. This program is a one-day session aimed at teaching many of the same principles that M.O.R.E. stressed. Every year, mandatory attendance was required by all of our athletes, support personnel, and coaches.

Dr. Don Schweingruber was responsible for formulating the structure and content of the program. Thanks to him, we were not only getting our athletes ready to compete in the upcoming game, but were also preparing them for the game of life. In addition, it reduced the number of referrals with which Don had to deal, and reduced my stress level.

Today, most NCAA I, II, and III schools provide a citizenship component as part of their program.

New Recruits

In the spring of 1983, a place kicker from The Netherlands, Hugo Sandberg, visited campus. Hugo was a foreign exchange student attending Bloom-Carroll High School, (Carroll, Ohio) near Lancaster. Before spending too much time with him, I decided to have him showcase his kicking skills. We proceeded to the practice field.

I had him kick a few extra points, which he made without much effort. Since almost any kicker can kick an extra point, I moved him back a few yards to try his foot at a field goal. At ten yards, he split the uprights; 20 yards, same thing; 40 yards.

I couldn't believe what I was seeing. Did we have a kicker?

I gave him one last test. I placed the ball some distance from the goal line and instructed him to kick-off. "Where do you want me to kick it?"

This was a first! Most of our past kickers were lucky to keep the ball in play, let alone place it.

There were some girls sunning themselves in bikinis behind Hirschy Annex (Neufeld Hall had not been constructed), so

I thought I would make it interesting, "See those girls sunning themselves? Can you put the ball among them?"

They were about 70 yards away, so I knew there was no chance of him kicking the ball that far. But, if he came within 15 yards, when he retrieved the ball Hugo would have an opportunity to gaze upon some bikini-clad coeds, and perhaps even meet one of them. What red blooded American, or Dutch, male doesn't like seeing members of the opposite sex in bikinis? At the time, this sounded like a good idea.

Hugo lined up about six yards from the ball and made a running start. When he made contact, it sounded like dynamite exploding. The ball shot off the tee and started to climb, and climb, and climb. This could be a problem! It reached its apex at about halfway to the girls, and started its descent. I couldn't believe my eyes! This ball had a chance of landing near them, or even worse, hitting one.

It did, in the midsection, but a bit lower, lower still. She didn't move! *Lord, he's killed her!*

I ran to the scene. By the time I arrived, she had recovered from having her breath knocked out, and was rolling from side-to-side in pain, "I'm so sorry. Are you OK?"

She seemed to be recovering, but understandably, she was not happy, "I'm telling President Neufeld on you, Coach Carpenter!"

That afternoon, the call came, "Carlin, this is Sue. President Neufeld would like to have a word with you. Are you free right now?"

I knew what this was about, but was hoping it might be concerning something else. I was tempted to say that I had a meeting to attend, and couldn't come now, but thought better of it.

I always had the greatest respect for President Neufeld. Many called him by his first name, Elmer, but I couldn't bring myself to do so. He seemed regal, almost angelic. When I arrived, he was sitting behind his desk; his demeanor did not convey happiness, certainly not angelic.

"Carlin, a young lady contacted me today and said you purposely had one of your players hit her with a *futball*." President Neufeld never pronounced the oblong object correctly. He always put a long "u" in it. "Is that correct?"

Thinking, I didn't really tell Hugo to hit her, only to put the ball among them, I replied. "No, I absolutely did not!" I sensed he knew I was splitting hairs, no pun intended, and proceeded to lecture me on the proper behavior expected from a member of the faculty.

I thanked President Neufeld for his time and left. Lesson learned!

A few years later, I told him I wasn't completely truthful about the kicking incident. He smiled, and confirmed what he suspected, "I know." I felt better!

Hugo became the most prolific kicker in the history of Bluffton College with ten kicking records. Also, he was first team NAIA District 22 in 1985 and 1986. Hugo was an NAIA Scholar-Athlete in 1984, 1985, and 1986. He graduated in 1987.

Dr. Elmer Neufeld was president of Bluffton College from 1978 to 1996. He passed away on March 30, 2009. He was the kind of person I hope to become.

Akron to Bluffton in Seven Hours

Recruiting on Saturday was always difficult. Usually the recruits were scheduled to arrive between 11:30 and noon, followed by lunch with some of our players, after which they were given a tour of campus, ending at the stadium, where I would meet with them and their parents. The worst case scenario would be if one came late and we had to extend our day; most times, our Saturday ended by 4 p.m.

We had scheduled Jesse Williams from Akron (OH) East High School, accompanied by his father, for a Saturday visit, with their arrival time at 11:30. Jesse did not arrive at 11:30. It wasn't unusual for a recruit to cancel his visit without notifying us, so we assumed that he was not coming. Much to our surprise, he arrived at approximately 3:30. This created a problem. Someone would have to stay in order to take him and his father to dinner, give them a tour of campus, and make a presentation outlining our program. Wanting to get my assistant coaches home with their families, I always took on this responsibility.

Normally when a recruit arrived this late, he had car problems. When I questioned Jesse about this, he assured me that he had not had any problems. I kept pressing him for an explanation as to why he arrived so late. "What time did you leave home?"

"We left at 7:30."

"Did you stop for an extended period?"

"We stopped for gas once, but otherwise came straight through."

"What route did you take?"

"We took interstate 71 to Cincinnati and 75 to Bluffton."

That explained why it took him seven hours to make the trip from Akron. I assured him that there was a shorter route for his return home and provided directions.

Jesse committed to Bluffton and started his freshman year at defensive back. He intercepted a Bluffton career-record 18 passes during 1985-88, with seven of those coming in 1987. Jesse earned All NAIA, District 22 honors in 1987 and 1988. During his tenure as a player, the Beavers went to the NAIA national playoffs for two consecutive years. Jesse was inducted into the Bluffton University Athletic Hall of Fame in 2012.

He graduated in 1989 and has spent his professional career with the Ohio Department of Rehabilitation and Corrections. Jesse is currently the director of the north region of the department's Office of Prisons. I often tell him, "I knew you would be in the prison system, but I thought you would have a number on your chest."

Jesse is also pastor of First Word Temple in Lima, Ohio. Sharon and I attended his ordination. Jesse and his wife, Lisa, reside in Lima with their three children. Each time we meet, I usually remind Jesse of his seven-hour trip to Bluffton with, "If you need any directions finding your way around Lima, call me."

Big League Chew

A recruit from Allen County, whom I'll call Craig, joined our team in 1985. I wasn't sure of his skills, but he was big and fast, or at least that is how his coach presented him to me on my recruiting visit to his school. For a running back, he was certainly big, but I had no idea about his speed. He played second string behind a player recruited by the Big 10 and therefore seldom appeared on film.

At any rate, I planned to recruit him based on his size. I arranged for Sharon and me to have dinner with Craig and his mother. Sharon was always helpful in recruiting in that she was able to relate to moms in a manner in which I couldn't. We had dinner at the Old Barn Out Back and made some progress, thanks to Sharon.

A couple of days later, I visited Craig's home. He was not present, but I had a nice visit with his mother. She and I talked on the front porch for nearly two hours. That was the only time I ever got sick on a home visit. It was during this time that I realized she chewed tobacco, plug.

Wanting to make a good impression, I bit off a big chunk of plug and began working it up. It wasn't long until I felt the effects of the nicotine. As a teenager, I had chewed tobacco many times, but it was always laced with licorice to give it a milder taste and mask the nicotine strength. Craig's mom chewed the real stuff, rolled leaf without licorice. By the time I left the visit, I had a splitting headache and ringing ears. I don't know if the size of my ears—they are big—had anything to do with the severity of the ring, but I couldn't hear.

I visited Craig's home many times before and during his career at Bluffton, and most times joined his mother in a chew, and became acclimated to the nicotine strength in her favorite tobacco. As a matter of fact, I became quite fond of our visits. I could chew and not catch hell from Sharon.

Noon Prayer

Tory Strock was a 6' 2", 210 pound quarterback whom we were recruiting from Liberty Center (OH) High School. During the recruiting process, Sharon and I visited with Tory and his family, and prior to the visit, he had informed me that he was favoring Ohio Northern University (Ada, OH). As a matter of fact, he had made a deposit there. This was common practice in that it indicated the student's intent to attend a particular school. If he did not attend, the deposit was forfeited. Once a deposit was made, normally the student-athlete was committed.

We had a great visit, and as usual Sharon charmed his parents; however, I had no illusions about getting him once a deposit was made at another institution. As always, I made a follow-up call the next day, and much to my surprise and delight, Tory was coming to Bluffton! I informed him that he was to call Ohio Northern and tell them of his decision.

Once he made the call, I knew that he was going to get a lot of pressure from Tom Kaczkowski, the head coach at ONU. Ohio Northern was on our schedule for the next two years, and Tom's final shot was, "Bluffton will never beat Northern!"

Although Tory had great athleticism, we felt that Darrin Fox was better suited to what we were doing offensively, so Tory was moved from quarterback to receiver. Although he was not totally happy with the move, Tory adjusted well to that position.

Tory was a starting player during his freshman year, but one of the many situations with which we had to deal was starting players thinking they could play at a higher level, and Tory was no exception. Obviously, if they were starting for us, we certainly did not want to lose them. Sure enough, during the spring of his freshman year, I received reliable information that he was planning to transfer to Bowling Green State University. Tory was good enough to play at that level, so he had a legitimate reason for leaving, but somehow I had to block his departure.

These were always delicate situations. I couldn't tell Tory he wasn't good enough to play at Division I. Instead, I had to confront him in a non-threating manner. The best plan I could come up with was to take him to lunch and perhaps he would reveal his intentions. Hopefully, it was just a false rumor.

We decided on the L&K Restaurant for lunch. We made small talk waiting for our meal to be served, but nothing was mentioned about his transferring. I knew that eventually I had to address the subject but didn't exactly know how.

Our lunch was finally served and I volunteered to say a prayer prior to our dining. Then it hit me! I will mention the rumor of his transferring in my prayer. I thanked God for the food, continued good health, Tory's presence at Bluffton College, his contribution to the football team, and closed with, "God, if Tory transfers, let this food which we are about to partake give him unrelenting diarrhea for the next six months. Amen."

Tory never flinched and we continued our visit over lunch. Transferring was never again mentioned during his remaining three years at Bluffton.

During Tory's sophomore year against Ohio Northern University, Darrin Fox, our quarterback, hooked up with him in the left corner of the end zone for a touchdown with only a few seconds remaining in the game. Fox then hit Gary Smiddy in the right flat for the two point conversion; Bluffton College 29, Ohio Northern 28 at ONU. That was the first victory over Northern since 1971.

Twice, Tory earned first team honors in the Association of Mideast Colleges (AMC). He graduated in 1997 and is a highly successful head football coach at Napoleon (OH) High School.

I often see Tory, and we always have a good laugh about our luncheon experience.

Tory married Cinda Creager, from Hamler, Ohio, and they have three children, Grant, Taylor, and Morgan. Sharon and I attended their wedding.

Player Relations

Vido Tatum, cousin of Ohio State's All-American Jack Tatum, who later played for the Oakland Raiders, was our starting tailback in 1981. Vido was from Cleveland Heights, Ohio, and was a tough kid. His friend, Kenny Hughes, was a quarterback from the same place. During lunch in Marbeck's dining hall, Kenny made a lewd remark about Vido's girlfriend, and Vido knocked him out, colder than a wedge.

Early one Sunday afternoon, Vido called and wanted to take a "bathe"—not bath, *bathe*—at our house. I questioned his motive and he informed me he didn't like the showers on campus and missed bathing, which was his custom on Sundays.

Well, he was my starting tailback, and my tub was empty, so why not? This was a first!

Vido arrived with Kenny and another friend. I inquired, "Are all of you going to take a bathe?" They assured me they weren't, only Vido.

While Vido took his bathe, Sharon and I served his friends soft drinks, cookies, and entertained them. After Vido finished, they thanked us, and departed.

At least once a year, Vido pays us a social visit. I still question his motive for wanting to take a bathe. I am convinced he bet his two friends he could take a bathe at the coach's house. He denies it.

The Nelsonville Duo

In 1981, Nelsonville-York High School won the Division III Football State Championship. There were two players on that team I wanted at Bluffton, Brad Woodson and Ross Flowers. Brad's mother, Georgianna Woodson, babysat me, and I had gone to school with Ross's parents, Gary Flowers and Dixie Dixon. I was confident I would get them, and my confidence was well founded; they both committed.

They arrived for two-a-day practices in Brad's van. Considering its mechanical condition, I had no idea how it was able to travel from Nelsonville to Bluffton. It looked like the kind of van from which one would remove the wheels, put the frame up on blocks, and use it as a chicken coop, which some did in Nelsonville.

Four days into fall practice, Mrs. Woodson called. "Brad and Ross are homesick and are thinking about leaving. Whatever you do, don't let them come home." I assured her I wouldn't let them leave, and prepared a plan to thwart their departure: I would remove the distributor cap from the van. Without a distributor cap, there was no way it would start.

I put my plan into action that night. After each day's practice, I would pass the parking lot where the van was parked. On two occasions, Brad and Ross were working feverishly under the hood, but to no avail. At the conclusion of preseason practice, I informed them of my deed. According to them, they knew the distributor cap was missing, but couldn't figure out what happened to it, and were unable to find a replacement in Bluffton.

Their homesickness finally passed, and each graduated. Both were outstanding defensive lineman and started on the 1985 team that finished 8 and 1.

***

Too Many Dogs and Cats

Without fail, every summer a player would call and inform me that he was not going to return to school. In the summer of 1984, a starting offensive lineman, whom I'll call Robert, from a rural Ohio town telephoned and said he wasn't returning. He was an important part of our offense, so I decided to make a personal visit to his home in an attempt to persuade him to change his mind. Sharon and I loaded up and headed east.

Robert lived in the outskirts of the town at the end of a dirt lane. Sharon and I arrived at his house and were greeted by a pack of five yapping dogs, one of which was a German Shepard. The other four were small and made a lot of noise, but otherwise, were harmless. The shepard was the only one that gave me some concern. The hair was raised on the back of his neck and his tail was tucked between his legs—not a good sign! I honked the horn and, thankfully, Robert called all the dogs into the house and motioned for me to enter. Sharon remained in the car.

Upon entering his home, my eyes started to burn from the ammonia fumes permeating the air, and then the unmistakable odor of urine and feces hit me. As I surveyed the dwelling, it was obvious why such stench was present. Along with the five dogs, there were about as many cats or more. The cats scurried about, so I couldn't get an accurate count. There were dog and cat feces throughout —on the kitchen table, furniture, and floor. Urine stains were ever present. Never have I encountered such a sickening environment.

After a brief visit, I departed. I couldn't stand it any longer!

When I returned to the car, Sharon asked, "What's the matter? You're white as a sheet!" I couldn't respond. At the end of the dirt lane, I stopped the car and vomited.

I never saw Robert again.

Steve?

Every June I sent out a summer conditioning program. Each player was to follow it before reporting to fall practice. At the end of every week, each player was instructed to return a progress report on the previous week's compliance.

A player I'll call Steve had not returned his report for a couple of weeks, and I became concerned about his commitment. Steve was our number two defensive back, and come fall, would play a major role on our defense. Concerned that he wasn't working out, I decided to pay him a personal visit.

I arrived at his home to be informed by his mother, "Steve doesn't stay here anymore." The fact that he didn't live at home anymore didn't sound good. Steve's mother gave me his address and I proceeded to the new location.

Upon arriving at his current address, I climbed the stairs of a grungy apartment building and found the door marked 201B, Steve's new address. I knocked, and a woman with shoulder length blond hair opened the door. She was dressed in a short skirt with matching blouse, plus stiletto heels. She was well built. Maybe Steve's decision to leave home wasn't such a bad idea after all!

I greeted her and introduced myself, "I'm Carlin Carpenter, head football coach at Bluffton College."

"I know who you are, Coach," was her response.

I recognized the voice. It was Steve! I departed and didn't bother to ask why he had not returned his workout card.

I hope he or she found happiness.

Tough Enough

College students are known for pulling practical jokes. It serves as a release from the rigors of college life, or so it is said. One of these pranks almost cost Darrin Gates, 6'4", 236 pound tight end from Shaker Heights, Ohio, his life.

Darrin was one of the best tight ends to ever play at Bluffton. He had great hands, but he only blocked when the spirit moved him, or when Coach Stokes threatened him with castration.

Louie Stokes, our offensive line coach, always wanted to bench him because of his blocking, or lack of. We had many staff meeting arguments over this matter. Louie always complained, "He is not tough enough!" Finally, I had had enough and informed Louie, "I need Darrin Gates more than I need you." After that, there were no more arguments over Darrin.

Darrin lived on the third floor of Lincoln Hall. As a prank, a sick one at that, a student sprayed Darrin's door with lighter fluid and set it ablaze, thinking that the lighter fluid would burn itself out, leaving the door undamaged.

But disaster stuck! The carpet in front of the door caught fire and started a chain reaction, causing the door facing to ignite. When Darrin's room filled with smoke, and he attempted to escape, he could not exit through the fire. Next best thing, jump! And he did, from the third floor of Lincoln Hall.

Darrin was already recovering from arthroscopic knee surgery to repair damaged cartilage, and luckily landed on wet, soft turf. Darrin then returned to the burning dorm, assisted a smoke-induced disoriented student to safety, and again returned to pull the fire alarm. The student he assisted from the dorm was the one who pulled the prank.

We sent Darrin to our orthopedic surgeon the next day, and he released him to play intramural basketball that night. Louie re-evaluated his perception of Darrin's toughness.

Darrin was a NAIA District 22 first team selection for three consecutive years: 1986, 1987, 1988.

Sly

Coach Homer McDuffie called and recommended Sylvester "Sly" Hubbard. He informed me that Sylvester was an outstanding player at Marion (OH) Harding High School but was a free spirit. I've heard coaches describe a player as a free spirit before and, when translated, it always means trouble.

Since Homer graduated from Bluffton, I felt obligated to contact Sylvester. He had great size, 6' 2", 210, and according to Sly, could run a 4.35 forty-yard dash. This speed in the forty was exceptional for a person his size, so I doubted his proclamation. I arranged for him to visit campus and he decided to continue his education here.

As I've metioned, each summer a workout package was sent to each recruit, and I would follow-up with a phone call to confirm each had received it. When I called Sylvester, he assured me he had received the workout, but wasn't going to follow it. He claimed he didn't need to, in that he was in better physical condition than any of my players.

Of course, this resulted in a heated verbal exchange. I told him he didn't need to report to fall practice, but he informed me he was coming anyway. I liked his brazen attitude, and hoped he would report. As one of my assistants, Louie Stokes, always contended, "You can't win championships with choir boys." I was looking forward to confronting him face-to-face.

Sylvester did report and was the most obnoxious, loud, disrespectful, angry person I had ever met. He was a take-home final for a PhD in clinical psychology, but I sensed he was intelligent. If I could channel this attitude into his play, he was going to be a great one.

Sylvester started as a freshman at linebacker. During his first year, he was more trouble than his contribution to the team was worth. Finally, I had had all I could stand and dismissed him for his sophomore season. Only if a player's behavior was detrimental to the team's success did I dismiss one permanently. I always contended that every person has the ability to change. Once dismissed, our program could no longer play a role in changing him. I took a lot of criticism from my staff for this position.

During the spring of his second year, Sylvester approached me with a request to be reinstated. He promised to do anything I would ask and play any position. James "Spike" Berry, a highly successful football coach at Cory-Rawson High School (Rawson, OH) and a Bluffton graduate, gave me some sound advice. "Put your fastest and best defender at defensive end, and play him to the wide side of the field."

Spike is the only coach I know who coached an undefeated team that was not scored on, so when he spoke, I listened. I wasn't sure Sylvester was our best defender, and his claim to run a 4.35 forty wasn't accurate, but he did run a 4.5, which is fast—really fast for his size.

I did as Spike suggested, and Sylvester found his position. He was devastating at defensive end. Nothing got around him! When the ball went the other way, Sly would run down the ball carrier from behind before he crossed the line of scrimmage, and he terrorized quarterbacks. This was his position, but his promise to conduct himself in an appropriate manner did not last long. He was still a problem.

About once a week, he would get into a fight at practice. During the first fight, I tried to separate the combatants and took an inadvertent elbow in the mouth. After that, with their helmets and equipment on, neither participant could hurt one another, so I would move the huddle and let them fight until one gave out.

To aggravate me, he would roll, yes roll, instead of running back to the huddle. The first time he did it, I let it slide, but the second time, I went berserk and started kicking him in the back as hard as I could. That put a stop to the rolling. If injured, he would not report to the trainer for treatment. He claimed that apples were the best cure for anything. Since he was a great player and an important part of our defense, I gave him apples. He never missed a practice or game because of injury. Apples!

Sylvester was having a dental problem, so I contacted Dr. Phillip Weisenbarger, a local dentist, and made an appointment. After he had seen Dr. Weisenbarger, the doctor called and informed me that Sylvester threatened to do him bodily harm if the good doctor caused him any pain. Dr. Weisenbarger thought he was nuts.

Sylvester wore glasses, but not in practice. When he wasn't wearing his glasses, he remained in a constant squint. I made an appointment for him to see Dr. Alan Yoder, a Bluffton optometrist. Dr. Yoder couldn't believe the results of the exam. He had a perforated retina in one eye and 20/200 vision in his good eye, which made him virtually blind. Dr. Yoder fitted him with new glasses for everyday wear and a pair of athletic glasses for football, no charge.

Sylvester and I argued violently throughout his junior year. Every week, I would have him report to my office to address his inappropriate behavior, which occurred both on and off of the field. Nothing ever got resolved. His behavior didn't change. I was determined to alter his attitude, and made it my personal goal to do so. One of us had to break, and it wasn't going to be me. I was relentless.

We would close each meeting with Sylvester claiming, "You can't make me do anything!"

I always came back with, "And you can't make me stop loving you."

In leaving, he would hit me with, "I hate you!"

As he left my office, I would give him a hug, which he detested.

Late in his senior year, Sylvester started to make the transition to becoming an upstanding citizen, and today is employed as an information technology professional in Charlotte, North Carolina. His work takes him all over the world. He has written a book titled, *Thoughts from Within.* He signed my copy, "Coach: A father, a friend, and a brother. I love you and your wife. Sylvester Hubbard."

Mr. Hubbard was selected NAIA District 22 first team in 1987 and 1988. He was chosen by his peers to give the baccalaureate address at his graduation. As he stood at the podium, I fought back tears.

I often talk to Sylvester, and when Sly is in town, he, Sharon, and I always have dinner together. We end our visits with hugs all around and, "I Love you and I mean it!"

We both won.

Toothless

Prior to each home game, the team always met at 8 a.m., followed by a pre-game meal. Greg Gilcrease, a 6 foot, 209 pound running back from Lima Senior High School was late for the meeting. Since Greg was a very important part of our offense, this was a major concern. He usually was good for 100 yards and a couple of touchdowns per game, so we needed him. Much to my relief, midway through the meal, he arrived.

I confronted him, "You are late! Where have you been?"

"I had to take my two-month old to the dentist."

During Greg's freshman year, often he was late, and usually had a weak excuse. Regardless of his reason for being late, I always punished him, which usually involved running. Some serious punishment was in order for this one.

"What did the dentist say about her teeth?"

"He said they were fine, no cavities."

"Greg, a two-month old doesn't have teeth! That will cost you a one-mile run after practice for the next three days. The next time you are late, you better buy a pair of track shoes. You will need them for all the running that will be in order."

Greg wasn't late again, at least not for a couple of weeks.

After his freshman year's success, I had an 8x10 picture of Greg framed, and placed it on the nightstand next to my bed. Every morning, I would look at his picture and think, *What can I do today to insure his graduation?* I knew, if he graduated, I would have him for four years. Greg graduated in 1989.

Greg was a first team selection, NAIA District 22 in 1986, 1987, and 1988. Also, he received All-America honors, once. Although not as good as Elbert Dubenion or Willie Taylor, he was close.

***

Psycho-Cybernetics

Monday mornings were always a flurry of activity. Via film, we evaluated each player's performance in the previous Saturday's game and gave him a grade, had a personnel meeting to determine if position changes were in order, finalized our scouting report on our upcoming opponent, and prepared the week's practice plan. The most important meeting occurred at 8 a.m.: injury report.

Each Monday morning, Phill Talavinia, our trainer, would deliver the verdict whether there was any player who sustained an injury in the past game that would not allow him to participate in next Saturday's contest? If there were any serious injuries, I could usually tell by Phill's demeanor the instant he entered the meeting.

He didn't look too good today, and his message wasn't any better, "Jeff is out for Saturday with a partial separation of the AC joint." Jeff Fortkamp was a 6 foot, 175 pound starting linebacker from Celina, Ohio.

"Are you sure he can't be ready by Saturday? That is six days! "

"Positive. He will never recover enough to play this week. As we speak, he is on his way to see Jeb." Dr. James "Jeb" Bagenstose was our team orthopedist.

An AC sprain involves the shoulder's acromion and clavicle bones, and when a traumatic blow forces them out of line, severe pain and lack of motion results. This was not good. I never questioned Phill's decision concerning whether a player would be physically able to play or not. His word was gospel. But we needed Jeff. He was one of our best linebackers and played a major role in stopping the run and was of utmost importance defending against the pass.

In 1960, Dr. Maxwell Maltz, MD, had written a self-help book titled *Psycho-Cybernetics*. In essence, it was a book describing how one's unconscious recesses could steer one in the right direction, including overcoming injury, pain, and illness.

A few years before, I had read this book. I informed Phill about the book and asked him for permission to give Dr. Maltz's psycho-cybernetics a try. Through his uncontrollable laughter, he gave me permission.

After Jeff returned from Dr. Bagenstose's office, I arranged a meeting with him. Jeff was open to the experiment and was ready to begin his recovery. In all honesty, I didn't remember much about the book, but I was going to put into practice what I thought I remembered. Admittedly, not particularly sound medical practice. I swore Jeff to secrecy for fear that the rest of the team and coaches would have me committed.

"Jeff, if you can get better by twenty percent each day, by Saturday you will be well. Agree?"

Not sounding overly convinced, he replied, "Your math is correct."

"Now Jeff, I want you to get treatment three times a day; heat, cold, and ultra sound. OK?"

"OK, Coach."

"Every hour, I want you to say to yourself, I'm getting better, ten times. OK?"

"OK, Coach."

"Each night, when you go to bed, I want you to say to yourself, I'm getting better, one hundred times. When you get up in the morning, I want you to say I'm twenty percent better. OK, Jeff?"

"OK, Coach."

"We will meet again tomorrow, same time and place. OK?"

"OK, Coach."

Jeff continued this routine for the week, and by Saturday, he was well. He played in Saturday's game and led the team in tackles—23.

I still remind Phill, "Never say never!"

Jeff was a first team NAIA District 22 selection in 1989 and 1990.

***

The (Almost) Fight

We were playing at Olivet (MI) College, and things weren't going well. Olivet scored just before the half. Our leading linebacker, Rob Hayden, had the flu and went to the bus between defensive plays to rest and get warm.

The touchdown prior to the half was a pass over one of our best defensive backs, Shawn Hertzfeld. Shawn, from Waterville, Ohio, was one of our most solid defenders. This poor coverage was not customary play for Shawn. He was a fearless competitor and took it personally when beaten. He showed little of this attitude today. I was not happy with his performance.

At half, we returned to the locker room to make adjustments. When I chastised Shawn about his poor performance, he became combative.

I shot back, "Rob Hayden has the flu, returns to the bus to rest when we have the ball, and is giving a better effort than you. Are you sick?"

"No, I'm not sick!"

"Well, your passive play is making me sick! You couldn't fight your way out of a wet paper bag!"

"I can whip your ass, old man!"

"Don't let your alligator mouth overload your humming bird ass. Step right up!"

With fire in his eyes, Shawn jumped up and headed my way. Fortunately, some of the players restrained him. I was happy for that. There was no way I could have whipped him. As a matter of fact, when he charged, I almost made a run for it; however, he would surely have caught me. I would have been exhausted from running and beaten-up.

We lost, 14-26.

I called Shawn's parents, Tom and Marilyn, Sunday morning and explained the situation. They informed me that Shawn and his long-time girlfriend had split. Oh, the power of a woman! Shawn and I restored our relationship, along with his great play. I'm waiting until he gets a little older to challenge him again.

Shawn was selected first team NAIA District 22 twice, in 1989 and 1990. Plus, he earned NAIA National Player of the Week honors once. Shawn was a competitor!

Shawn's sister, Tara, served on our athletic training staff. Tara died on October 27, 1992, after a two-and-a-half-year battle with cancer. On November 2, we honored her memory with a memorial service in Founders Hall.

Shawn and Tara were a positive testimony to Tom's and Marilyn's parenting.

In 1989 and 1990, Rob Hayden, Belle Center, Ohio, received first team NAIA District 22 honors. Sadly, a few years after graduating, Rob was killed in an auto accident on his way to work. He had one of the most uplifting personalities of any person I have ever known. He always made people feel good about themselves.

I cried at Tara's and Rob's funerals.

The Wedding

Often when a player married, Sharon and I would receive an invitation to attend. We went to as many weddings as time would allow, and if we couldn't appear, we would send a gift.

Chris Dales, an offensive guard from Defiance, Ohio, sent us an invitation. Chris was one of our best players—first team NAIA District 22 in '88, '89—and we had become close to his family, who never missed a game. We welcomed the invitation and looked forward to attending his wedding.

After the wedding, a reception followed with an abundance of food and beverages. As the night wore on, it was time for a brief dance with the bride and groom. Of course, one had to pay for the privilege, which added to their honeymoon coffers. The women in attendance would dance with the groom, and the men with the bride, as is customary at most weddings.

I didn't really know the bride, but I knew the groom well. I cut-in and danced with Chris, leaving the bride standing. I felt it was necessary to inform Chris of some pitfalls he might encounter in marriage. Having been married forever, I was certain I was qualified to get him off to a good start, saying, "If there are any quirks that Shellie has that irritate you, in ten years, multiply that irritation by 1000. And you may want to be prepared for having her tell you your shirt doesn't match your pants and proceed to change your wardrobe. Also, get used to saying, 'You're right honey, I'm sorry.'"

I was about to give him some tried-and-true tips about sex, but before I could enlighten him, Sharon cut-in for her dance. He never contacted me for any additional nuggets of marriage wisdom, so I assume he figured the sex thing out.

As head football coach at Ayersville High School, Defiance area, Chris invited me to address his team prior to a state playoff game. I enjoyed the occasion and was honored that he thought of me at such an important milestone in his program.

English Paper

All the freshmen football players had to attend study table their first term. Study table ran from 7 p.m. until 10 p.m. Monday through Thursday. Each coach took turns monitoring these study session. After the first term, we would check grades, and if the player had a cumulative 2.5 GPA or better, he was excused and could study on his own. At midterm, we would check all upperclassmen's grades and would assign those with lower than a 2.25 GPA to study table. If a player was struggling in a course, the study table monitor would tutor him.

Tyson Goings, our starting running back, was having trouble in freshman English. Like many first-year students, college was more demanding than high school in that there were considerably more readings required as well as composition assignments. Tyson had received poor grades on the first few papers he had written, so I decided to assist him with his next writing assignment. I felt confident we could raise his grade on the next paper. Being an undergraduate psychology major, I had written many papers and did well on them. Plus, I had written a 145-page thesis for my master's degree and was tri-author of a scientific paper published in *Turtox News* titled "Inexpensive Double Diffusion Method for Biology Projects." With my expertise in writing, I knew we could compose an A, or at minimum, a B+ paper.

We spent the next couple of weeks writing and rewriting the paper. I would edit Tyson's work and then help him rewrite it. When we finished, the paper was a masterpiece worthy of a Pulitzer.

Tyson was really proud of our accomplishments and submitted the paper a day before it was due.

Grade = D. In my opinion, this freshman English class should have been a graduate level course. Tyson never asked me to help with another paper, nor did I volunteer my services.

For three years, he was first team Heartland Collegiate Athletic Conference (HCAC) and in 2000 was voted by the conference coaches as Player of The Year, and was All-America Honorable Mention.

Tyson graduated in 2001 with a major in recreation management. He has also completed his master's degree in professional counseling, and serves as dean of students at Lima Senior High School.

Coach Relations

I consider Dick Strahm, a good friend. Dick was the coach of the Findlay (OH) College Oilers. He had some great teams, none of which we ever defeated. Early on I looked forward to playing his teams, but soon discovered we were not able to compete on the same level. For one thing, his facilities were much more accommodating than Harmon Field, which made it difficult to recruit the same caliber of athletes.

Whenever Findlay came to Bluffton, each team dressed on campus, and then Dick would bus his players to the field. We would walk. Immediately prior to the game and at half-time, we all assembled in a shed staging area that was worse than any chicken coop. Both teams were side-by-side with each separated by a paper thin wall. There was no heat or restroom facilities, and only enough room to seat half of the team at a time. The rest remained outside.

A few minutes prior to kickoff, Dick and I would meet behind the structure to relieve the pressure on our bladders. Standing together, we would urinate in the weeds, all the while discussing today's game, and wondering if the head coaches at Ohio State and

Michigan were sharing this same intimate moment prior to their contest.

I recall once when Dick asked if I had received his roster, I responded, "I already took it from the FBI's most wanted list off the bulletin board in our post office." The half-time score of that game was FC 42, BC 0. After that, I never cracked any more jokes about his team.

Coach Strahm has since retired and was inducted into the National Football Foundation and College Hall of Fame. His teams won four NAIA National Championships; however, we are equals in that both of our kidneys are functional (allowing for that kidney stone that Sharon slapped out of me).

On our twenty-fifth wedding anniversary, Dick sent me a poster-picture of his team with the scores of all the times that the Oilers had defeated us. He signed it, "Thanks for the memories." I still haven't forgiven him.

Rain Men

During a game at Anderson (IN) it rained all day; steady, incessant rain. To make matters worse, we lost after leading most of the game. Everybody was cold and wet. All were looking forward to some hot food and drink. On our way out of town, we stopped at McDonald's.

My assistant coaches, Greg Brooks, Ed Stults, Don Bauer, and some other support personnel, rode to the game in a van driven by Arman Habegger. Arman, with his passengers, arrived ready to eat. The place was packed with our party and other customers.

Before boarding the bus and van for home, I needed to give Greg some details about Monday's meeting, and requested for Arman to get him. The restaurant was still crowded and Arman went to find him amid the chaos. He returned and reported, "I can't find Greg."

"Well, then get Ed."

Arman searched and came back, "I can't find Ed, either!"

"Didn't both ride with you from the stadium?"

"No."

"You mean you left them at the stadium?"

"No, I didn't leave them; they forgot to get in the van."

"Arman, isn't it reasonable...?" I stopped. I was going to say, "Isn't it reasonable that since they rode with you, they would return with you?" I knew if I brought "reason" into the equation, it would only agitate Arman. He is easily agitated; besides, I didn't feel like arguing with him.

We returned to the stadium to find that the custodial personnel had locked the facility, and both Greg and Ed, along with Don, were standing outside in the rain, soaked and cold. Arman had forgotten them.

On the return trip to Bluffton, Arman took a barrage of abusive comments from the three. Arman, remembering how we had lost in the closing minutes of the game, finally shot back, "Let's talk about why we lost the game!" That put a stop to the others badgering him. He still claims it was their fault that they missed their ride.

If You Build It...

Bluffton needed its own stadium and a fairy tale ending like that of "The Three Little Pigs." Most of our opponents had an on-campus stadium or played in a high school stadium much larger than Harmon Field, which we shared with the local school. In addition, we had to walk five blocks to get there. Most recruits' high school stadiums were better than ours.

Whenever I had the opportunity, I lobbied anybody who would listen about our need for a new structure. Finally, in 1984, the administration decided it was time to start researching the feasibility of building an on-campus stadium. That was all I needed!

In '84 our final record was 2-7. I was in the second year of a two-year contract and on shaky ground. If I was going to remain at Bluffton, we needed to have an exceptional year, and that depended on the strength of the 1985 recruits. In order to help insure a strong class, I brought the prospect of a new stadium into the recruiting process.

I searched all of the trade magazines for a stadium that would meet our needs. I found several that I liked, and one caught my eye. It seated 10,000 and had a glass press box stretching the length of the structure. It was a beaut! Hey, if we were going to build one, it was going to be a good one.

I had the picture enlarged, and framed so recruits could see it. This was going to be similar to our new stadium; ours woud have seats and a press box, as did the one pictured...but not as *exactly* pictured. I did not share that tidbit with the recruits, leaving them to believe that the picture was an accurate representation of our planned stadium.

"It could be completed by your senior year," I told recruits and their parents when we met. "The new facility would have meeting rooms, locker rooms, a concession stand, seats with backs, and restrooms."

"The Three Little Pigs" is a complete fabrication, but it has an element of truth: it is wise to build one's house out of structurally solid material. The only element of truth in my stadium presentation was that we would have a new home.

As a result of my stadium promise, Bluffton experienced the best recruiting class in years. We had 106 players report for fall practice, with 53 of them freshmen. (We actually had 62 first-timers report, but lost 9 during two-a-days.) At some point during their stay at Bluffton, thirteen of the 53 were awarded first team NAIA District 22 Honors, some more than once. One played professionally in Europe and two were All-Americans.

From 1985 through 1988, the Beavers went on a run of 32 wins and 7 losses, were ranked nationally each year, and appeared twice in the NAIA National Playoffs, winning a playoff game for the first time in school history. Also, a combined 75 team and individual records were broken during this period. The 1985, 1987, and 1988 teams have all been inducted into the university's Athletic Hall of Fame.

Had I done a better job coaching, we would have accomplished more.

I recruited on the prospect of a new stadium for eight years, and in 1993, it became a reality. When the players, who were recruited from 1985 to 1992, return to campus, they sarcastically thank me for our new home. "You're welcome," is always my reply.

"The Three Little Pigs"—I love that fairy tale!

The 1985 Canadian Gold Rush

Financial aid was an important factor in determining whether a recruit was going to attend Bluffton. We offered no athletic grants, so what a player received depended on his financial need. There was some academic grant money available, but most students and/or their parents were still left with a hefty financial responsibility.

By chance, I learned that international students received some form of tuition wavier. I checked it out with the director of financial aid, and sure enough, they did. I knew they didn't play American football in Kenya or Somalia, but they did in Canada. They played 12-man football there, and the game wasn't as popular as it is in the U.S.A; however, it was still football.

Canadians John and Ross Weber, brothers, played under Kenny Mast, and both were great players. If I could recruit a couple like them, I would be in business. Tuition was a big chunk of the expense to attend Bluffton and Canadians were considered international students, so I headed north. I had struck gold!

I contacted every high school in Canada that played football and was able to get six to commit: two running backs, one offensive tackle, one defensive back, one defensive end, and one defensive tackle. All on tuition waivers!

The defensive tackle, Marcel Sterk, was 6'1" and 310 pounds. Marcel was big enough to have his own zip code, and he could run.

During specialty period, we always practiced our kickoffs and returns. We had five different kickoffs: zoom, kangaroo, squib, Alley Oop, and blast. On blast, the kicker would try to hit a player on the return team's front line, hoping the ball would ricochet off him and we would recover it.

Marcel was on the return team's front line and Hugo Sandberg was our kicker on the kickoff team. Marcel wasn't paying attention, so I instructed Hugo to blast him. He did! A line drive in the family jewels! Marcel hit the ground as if he were shot and remained there until finally revived by our trainer. From that point on, we had Marcel's undivided attention during kickoffs.

During my tenure, that was the last year that Canadians received a tuition waiver. The administration shut down my gold mine.

$250,000 Dog Bite

Dwight Salzman loved Bluffton College. He and his wife both attended here and often returned to their alma mater. For 21 years, Dwight taught physical education and coached track at Greenville (OH) High School. Whenever I was recruiting in Greenville, I would visit with him and his wife, Hazel, and I always looked forward to the visit. The only drawback to fully enjoying my time with them was the behavior of their dog. Knowing Dwight and Hazel were major contributors to the college, I could tolerate the mutt; besides, Dwight always told interesting stories, and I appreciated the history lesson.

During my early visits to Dwight's, the dog would make an appearance, sniff my leg, and move on. I appreciated his lack of interest in that he was the ugliest dog I had ever encountered—and the smelliest. He had an open sore on his right rib cage that he kept aggravating with his constant scratching. It appeared to me he had mange, caused by parasitic mites. His tail curled up over his back like a pig's, constantly exposing an unsightly posterior. He was short haired with a face like a bulldog on a terrier's body. Obviously, he was not AKC registered. Dwight told me his name on my first visit, but I forgot it. I mentally referred to him as Scab, after the sore on his side.

Following several visits, and much to my chagrin, the dog took a liking to me. The instant I would sit down, he would jump on my lap and stand. He was about two feet tall, and would look me in the face when I was conversing with Dwight, and when Dwight would respond, turn and face Dwight. His breath would run a buzzard off a gut wagon, and his posterior was even worse. When his side would aggravate him, he would sit and scratch with his right hind leg at the speed of a jack hammer, spewing hair and dead skin all over my lap and chest. Unfortunately, on this visit, I was wearing a new Navy, pin-striped suit. All through our conversation, around and around Scab would go, stopping only to scratch.

I had to come up with a plan to get Scab off my lap, so I requested a glass of water. When Dwight departed to the kitchen for Hazel to draw my water, I swatted the mongrel up along the side of his head. As he cleared my lap, I caught him in mid-air with my foot in his Vidalia onions. He gave out a yip, did a half gainer, lit on his back, righted himself, and scurried behind the couch. Dwight returned with the water and we continued our conversation, without mention of Scab's whereabouts.

When our visit had concluded, I thanked Dwight and Hazel for their hospitality and proceeded to the back door. As customary, after each visit, Dwight would walk me to the back door, which exited to his porch. The porch was approximately three feet off the ground and was accessible by three concrete steps. I would always stand on the bottom step, with Dwight positioned on his porch.

Prior to my departure, we would exchange pleasantries and bid farewell with a handshake. As I extended my hand, Scab came screaming out the back door, cleared the porch with two bounds, and sank his canines into my thigh, punching four holes in my new suit and as many puncture wounds in my leg. He then casually walked back inside.

Elephants and dogs remember.

Dwight was the impetus behind BC's Athletic Hall of Fame,

and half of a 1992 bequest of more than $250,000 from his estate was used to construct a new stadium. Because of Dwight's and Hazel's vision and generosity, Bluffton College played its first on-campus football game in its own stadium on September 11, 1993.

Thank you Dwight, Hazel, and Scab.

Beavers on the Road

Prior to 1985, the Bluffton Beavers traveled without travel bags. The players would pull their jerseys over their shoulder pads, turn them upside down, and place the rest of their gear in the jersey, then put it in the bus's cargo area for the trip. This style of packing did little to secure the gear for the bumpy bus ride that followed. When we arrived at our destination, loose equipment would be scattered everywhere.

Travel bags cost $50 each. Our budget could not stand $50 times 100. I had to stop the complaining, so I promised them team bags, but I didn't say what kind.

I called the Bluffton Grain Elevator to see if they had any type of bag that could serve the purpose. They did—burlap sacks. Perfect! I purchased one hundred, 100-pound bags for $1 each. That was a savings of $4,900.

The logo on half of the bags read, "Purina Hog Chow," and the other half, "Checkerboard Chicken Feed." They all needed draw strings, so I contacted Barbara Stettler, chair of our Home Economics Department and our team dietitian, to see if she could have some of her students sew them in. She agreed. Now all I had to do was sell the idea of burlap travel bags to everybody.

Before I sprung the new bags on the team, I told them the story about Dolly Parton's song, "Coat of Many Colors." When Dolly was a child, her mother crafted Dolly a coat from colorful rags, and regardless of what others said about it, Dolly knew it was sewn with love in each stitch. I compared the work of Ms. Stettler's students to Mom Parton's.

Finally, I presented the new bags. It didn't go well. The song was released in 1971, so most of them had never heard of it, or even Dolly Parton. They showed little enthusiasm for their new containers. I assured them, "These are just temporary. We will be getting new ones next year." Not true. I had no plans for any such purchase, but I had to ward off being drawn and quartered.

Over the next four years, the Beavers had the best record in the seventy-year history of Bluffton College football. The bags became the team's trademark. When we unloaded our bags at an opponent's stadium, we were greeted with hog and chicken calls. After a good trouncing by the Burlap Beavers, the opposing fans were silent.

We did finally purchase legitimate travel bags in 1989, but the players were reluctant to give up the burlap. They enjoyed the attention the bags generated.

The Funeral

In 1988, we won our first six games and were preparing for our seventh at Hanover College. Hanover was a tough opponent, especially at home. No Bluffton team had ever defeated Hanover on their own field.

In preparation for the matchup, I had to figure out some way to change our approach to that week's practice. After much debate with my staff, we decided to have a funeral to bury the ghost of Hanover, in hopes of exorcising the jinx they seemed to have on us.

Actually, I made the final decision to have a funeral. My coaches didn't think much of the idea.

I contacted Dr. J. Denny Weaver, professor of religion, to see if he would officiate the funeral ceremony. He agreed. Then, I went to the campus theater storage area and got a cardboard casket, secured a mannequin from a local clothing store, and dressed it in a makeshift Hanover uniform. Now, we needed a drummer, and one volunteered from the music department.

In preparation for the funeral, we loaded the "dead" Hanover player, representing the ghost of Hanover, in back of my Dodge station wagon. The processional started at the edge of the practice field, led by the drummer playing a mournful beat behind the hearse. Preacher Denny and the rest of the team followed. We proceeded to the center of the practice field, where we sang "Amazing Grace," and concluded the service with a moving eulogy by Deacon Weaver. We buried the jersey of the ghost of Hanover in a grove of trees adjacent to the field, erected a cross inscribed, "RIP - The Ghost of Hanover," and started practice.

The coaches and players thought I had finally crossed over to cuckoo!

Feeding the Multitudes

Whenever we traveled to Hanover, we would always stop at a roadside rest stop along the way. There were restroom facilities on the bus, but a stretch was in order about two hours into the trip. Along with the stretch, we would partake of a sack lunch. Each member of the traveling party was provided with two peanut butter and jelly sandwiches, a bag of potato chips, and an apple, plus a can of Coke or bottle of water. Phill Talavinia was responsible for making sure the food was ordered from Marbeck dining hall and the supplies loaded on the bus.

I yelled, "Lunch! Come and get it!" The players got in line for their meal.

As Phill and I were passing out the sacks of food, I noticed, with over half of the team yet to feed, that we only had a few bags left. Problem! Phill had forgotten half of our sacks of food! I wasn't happy, but didn't say anything. I stored the incident in my memory bank for future reference to counter any criticism Phill might make of me— "Yeah, but I didn't forget twenty-five sack lunches!"

I informed the team of the situation and that they would have to share. They complied, and there was food left over.

The Race

The trip to Hanover is a long one, the better part of four hours. Early in the trip, some would sleep, study, or watch a movie on the four television monitors located strategically in the bus. Early on I had allowed the players to choose the movie they wanted to see, but what they normally selected wasn't appropriate, so I chose now. I drew the line when they wanted to see *Debbie Does the Dallas Cowboys*.

A couple of hours into the trip, the players always became restless. Someone would make a disparaging remark about someone's athleticism or his girlfriend, and an argument would ensue. Sometimes, I would start an argument just to stir things up.

Gerald Johnson, a defensive back, was always running his mouth about something. On this particular trip, he was challenging me to a race, claiming he could give me a 10-yard head start, and still beat me in a 40-yard dash. Linebacker Bruce Gardner chimed in and would cover all bets, claiming, "Coach will burn Gerald in the race."

With the vote of confidence from Bruce, I made the first bet, $5. My bet started a frenzy of betting, some on me and some for Gerald. The race was set prior to our Friday walk-through on Hanover's game field. Bruce would start the race with, "On your mark, get set, go!"

Prior to the race, Bruce pulled me aside and gave me some

important instructions. "Just before I say 'go', I will flick my right foot. When I flick my foot, you go. I will follow with the start command close enough to the foot-flick so that no one will know you started early." I liked the plan.

I beat Gerald by 12 yards. I gained 2 yards on him and could have outrun him from an even start—with Bruce's help of course.

Bruce and I split $42.

Oh Lord! Why me?

The Hanover game was always an overnight trip and we usually departed on Friday at noon. When traveling to Hanover, we always stayed at the Clifty Inn, a part of Clifty Falls State Park, outside of Madison, Indiana. Clifty is a resort park to which countless people travel to admire the fall foliage and the inn was usually booked to capacity this time of year, October. The inn is two stories and shaped like a horseshoe around an Olympic swimming pool.

For our team, we always reserved the top floor, facing the swimming pool. During this time of year, the pool was always crowded with guests catching the last days of warmth prior to colder weather.

Before any game, I was always on edge and would lose my patience with the players over something that normally wouldn't bother me. So, whenever we stayed overnight, I always made sure my room was as far away from the players as possible. This location would separate me from them so that I wouldn't overreact to some innocent behavior that would cause me to do or say something I would later regret. The 1988 team was a rambunctious lot and had me on the verge of suicide most of the time.

After the four-hour trip to Hanover and the walk-through practice, a nap was always in order before dinner. Prior to reporting to my room, I informed the manager not to disturb me, unless there was a murder, until it was time for dinner. I lay down and started vegetating.

Knock, knock!

I went to the door. "I told you not to disturb me unless there was a murder."

"I know, Coach, but they locked Jamal out of his room and won't let him back in."

This behavior was common with this bunch. On every overnight trip, someone got locked out of his room and would have to beg to get back in.

In disgust, I replied, "So what? Every overnight trip someone gets locked out."

"But this time it is different, Coach."

"Why?"

"Because there are a lot of people around the pool."

"So?"

"He's naked."

"Naked!?"

"Yes, Coach, naked."

"Oh Lord! Why me!"

By the time I scrambled to the scene, Jamal (whose name was not really Jamal) was back in his room. I threatened the perpetrators with death and had the entire team locked down until dinner.

It didn't end there. When checking out the next day, I discovered our bill included phone calls over $200. One was to England! I forgot to have the phones turned off in the rooms.

On game day, it was all worth it: Bluffton 40, Hanover 21. It was the first game ever won by Bluffton at Hanover.

Happy Birthday with a Sippy Cup

When the team traveled overnight, we always ate Friday's evening meal at Ponderosa. The meal was within our budget and the traveling party could eat all they wanted—and they could eat! Regardless of Ponderosa's net daily profit, they had a deficit after we satisfied the locusts' appetite of the team.

Jon Spradling was a 5'5", 138 pound wide receiver form Sidney, Ohio. Although Jon was small, he played like he was 6'5 and 238 pounds. He had exceptional speed and could catch anything close. Besides, he had a great personality and the players gravitated to him. He was also mischievous, so whenever there was an opportunity to get one over on him, his teammates took the opportunity.

On his first road trip, following the meal at Ponderosa, the restaurant staff sang "Happy Birthday" to Jon and presented a cake. I didn't realize it was his birthday, and took the opportunity to offer my congratulation. With some hesitation, he replied, "It's not my birthday, Coach." Of course this followed with high fives among his teammates.

At every Ponderosa, someone would inform the restaurant's staff of Jon's "birthday" and a cake would follow. On several occasions, they would sit him in a booster chair with a Sippy cup, followed by a rousing chorus of "Happy Birthday." Jon always took it in stride, and each overnight trip, I looked forward to seeing how his teammates were going to celebrate his coming into this world.

Jon played a major role in the Beavers winning a share of the Heartland Collegiate Athletic Conference title in 2000 and was selected first team HCAC in 2001.

Hotel Blues

Immediately after the last game, the staff would go on an outing to celebrate the end of the season. If the last game was home, we would go that Saturday; if away, we would take the trip the following Saturday. Most times, we would go to Windsor, Canada, or Greek Town in Detroit to the casinos. None of us were high rollers, but we did enjoy playing the penny slots, reasonable food prices, and the camaraderie shared during the trip.

Prior to each outing, different members of the group were responsible for one phase of the adventure. Someone would rent a van, another make dinner reservations for on the way up, one for our dining there, one was responsible for where we ate on our return trip, and someone would make our hotel reservations. There were five couples who made the trip, so travel responsibilities would be the task of a spouse from each couple.

One year, the group consisted of Herb and Connie Purton, Phill and Michelle Talavinia, Roger and Erika Snyder, Louie and Melanie Stokes, plus Sharon and I. Roger was not a member of my staff, but he and Erika were friends of Louie and Mel. Any friends of the Stokeses were our friends, so they were invited. Roger had worked as an assistant for Louie in high school.

We chose Greek Town to unwind, and things were going smoothly. Around 3 a.m., we had had about as much fun as we could stand, so decided to call it a day. This year, Louie was responsible for making the hotel reservations, so we requested that he call the hotel to inform them we were on our way. He did so and proudly informed us, "Our beds are turned down with a mint on each pillow."

The hotel was several miles from the casino, so we didn't arrive until 3:45. All of us were ready to retire.

Upon arriving at the hotel, we unloaded our luggage and made our way to the hotel lobby. Louie led the way. As Louie presented himself to the attendant and requested keys, the clerk informed him, "I'm sorry, but I don't have a reservation for your group."

"What? I just called a few minutes ago and confirmed them."

"Sir, I did not receive a call from anybody in the last hour."

Now Louie is agitated, and the travel party was agitated at Louie. Louie explodes, "I'm telling you, I just talked with you and confirmed the reservation."

The clerk maintained his composure, "Sir, you did not call here!"

Louie whipped out a paper with the hotel's number on it. "If this isn't your number, I'll eat it!"

"Sir, you may want some ketchup with that, because you called the Comfort Inn's number, which is two blocks down the street;

this is Days Inn."

Red-faced and mumbling expletives under his breath, Louie followed the party back to the van for a reload. We verbally abused him all the way to the Comfort Inn and continued berating him for the remainder of the trip. As a matter of fact, whenever he mentions a mistake any of us has made, the hotel reservation fiasco quickly enters into the conversation.

We never again allowed Louie to make any reservations. None!

Wake Up!

Tyson Goings, Clint Fox, and Greg Ditz were a trio that nearly drove me into early retirement. They weren't inherently bad, but were always getting into some kind of mischief. They were all starters with great personalities and infectious laughs. One couldn't help but like them, but they were always up to something, which always kept me on my toes.

The team traveled to Barcelona, Spain, in 2001, for a 14-day cross-cultural experience and to play the Fenix Granollers. In addition to the game, the trip included service work, guided tours of historic Spanish sites, and a cruise on the Mediterranean Sea. We also visited Madrid and took guided tours of Toledo, Tossa de Mar, and Segovia.

There were 105 members in the group, which included students taking the trip for academic credit, coaches, coaches' wives, parents, and institution chaperons, Dr. Mary Ann Sullivan, Sally Reeder, and Jose Torres. Sally and Jose spoke the language, and Dr. Sullivan served as our art historian. She knew art! Also, Mrs. Reeder and her husband, Richard, once had a summer home in Barcelona and knew the area.

In Barcelona, the party stayed in a hotel near the beach and tourist area. I had no curfew and, after the day's activities, allowed the participants freedom to explore the area. Most of their free time was spent on the beach; it was topless. The only rule was that they had to be at breakfast by 7 a.m. Many would just be returning at seven and had to pay the price of fatigue, and whatever else was ailing them, for the remainder of the day.

One particular morning, Goings, Fox, Ditz and a young woman I'll call Jane were absent from breakfast. Jane was a student taking the course for credit. Phill and I made our way to their room. Upon arriving, the three Musketeers were asleep in three single beds located on the wall opposite the entrance and Jane, fully clothed, was bunked in a single just inside the door. Later, she informed me that she was locked out of her room and sought refuge in the nearest vacant bed. Knowing Jane, I believed her.

All were having sweet dreams of the previous night, but they were about to get a rude awakening. I quietly told Phill to slip into the bathroom, get the biggest towel he could find, fold it in half, wet the folded end, and bring it to me. Tyson was sleeping peacefully. I swung the wet towel with the force of a tennis racket and unloaded on him with a full serve. As Clint started to stir, I gave him the same medicine. Greg was still out, but not for long. I saved the last blast just for him, and when the towel hit its mark, he fell out of bed.

Jane was watching the activity with shock and awe, and as I approached her, she made a break for the door. The full force of a blow landed on her backside as she exited into the hall. I declared, "You all have three minutes to get to breakfast." Some fast dressing followed, and they made it, but their appetites weren't at full capacity. I'm not sure if their suppressed appetites resulted from the towel-beating, or what they had consumed the previous night.

For the remainder of the trip, no one was ever late for breakfast.

Mary Ann and Sally were involved in the pre-game ceremonial coin toss, and the Beavers prevailed, 28 to 0. Tyson was selected as the game's most valuable player.

It was a wonderful experience for all but one, who was not happy with the extent of freedom I had allowed the group and stated so in a letter to Ms. Elaine Suderman, assistant director of the cross-cultural program. However, Dr. Sullivan followed up with a letter to Ms. Suderman endorsing the way I managed the trip. I appreciated her support.

We returned safely with 105; no one was lost or injured.

Tyson, Clint, and Greg all were selected First Team HCAC numerous times. I am glad they were on our team!

Horseplay and Song

Every practice was different. Before each session, we would prepare a detailed plan on the area of concentration for that day. If we were going to have a productive day, I could usually tell by the attitude of the players during our stretching period. This day the players were acting strangely. There was a lot of whispering and stifled giggling. It provoked me so I put a stop to it, only to have this puerile behavior surface again during the team session. We were undefeated and well into the season, so I didn't think the team was about to mutiny.

Everything seemed to be centered on Dawn Henderson. Dawn was one of our student trainers. She was a good worker and well-liked. A trainer was assigned to each coach, and Phill Talavinia had assigned Dawn to me. Each coach's trainer would stay with that coach for the entire season.

Normally, the trainers would dress in sweat pants or jeans for practice. This was an unusually warm day, so most were wearing shorts; however, Dawn was in a knee-length winter coat. A lot of our support personnel would come to practice straight from class, and be dressed in "street" clothes. Some were doing their student teaching and would come in their finest attire. Knowing this, I didn't give Dawn's long coat a second thought; only that she had to be uncomfortably warm.

Most of the time, Dawn would be on the sideline with the other trainers, but today she kept standing a few feet behind me, and about half way through practice, yelled, "Coach!"

I was in the middle of chastising a player for a mistake he had made, and barked, "Wait a minute!"

She addressed me again, only louder, "Coach!"

I turned around. She seductively opened her coat to reveal a scanty bikini, and I mean scanty! It may have been painted on her.

I fell on my back, grabbed my chest, and yelled, "Heart attack!"

The team broke into uncontrollable hysterics. For the remainder of the practice, we didn't get much accomplished.

"The Administrative Staff, Plus One"

Prior to the start of fall classes in 1988, the faculty would participate in a carry-in dinner. Usually, the meal was followed by a few announcements and some form of entertainment provided by faculty members. Each year someone would volunteer to entertain.

A few years after my meeting with the administrative staff concerning my continued employment and/or termination, I was trying to come up with something to "bust their chops." This would be my opportunity, so I volunteered to make a presentation. What I came up with couldn't be too offensive, had to be entertaining, and should carry a message.

I spent some time evaluating the situation and decided on composing a song poking fun at them. There was a new academic dean, but he wasn't exempt. I titled it "The Administrative Staff, Plus One." The "One" was Harvey Hiebert. Harvey was our librarian. I always felt that Harvey took himself too seriously, so I planned to loosen him up.

Whenever I took a recruit on a tour of the library, I had to be careful what was said about the facility for fear Harvey would hear me. If I told the recruit that there were 10,000 volumes in the library, which also includes fifty study stations, and if it wasn't accurate, Harvey would send me a scathing note of correction: "The library has 10,001 volumes with fifty and one-half study stations. There is half a study station on the lower level that seats one small person."

I spent a few days composing "The Administrative Staff, Plus One," and after dinner cranked up my Martin guitar and hit the administrators, faculty, and guests with it:

> *I've written a song and it's not very long*
> *But it's got a message to say*
> *It's about a few, who lead us through*
> *And we always follow their way.*

Spoken:
> *The administrative staff, plus one.*

Chorus:
> *The administrative staff, they're quite a bunch*
> *They meet every Thursday for lunch*
> *When they get through, they go home at two*
> *And leave all the work for me and for you.*

> *Paul King is on the road every day*
> *Trying to raise our pay*
> *But when he comes home, he's broke and alone*
> *'Cause he ain't got no money and he knows he can't stay.*

Spoken:
> *Got to collect on all those pledges, Paul.*

Chorus

Fred Amstutz is a recruiter they say
And at night he puts up hay
But when recruiting is done
We're always short some
Because most can't afford to pay.

Spoken:

We need more campus visits, Fred.

Chorus

Don Schweingruber, oh what a name
No two pronounce it the same
He works in Riley Court, and he's awfully short
But we still love him just the same.

Spoken:

Will someone push the up button on Don's elevator shoes?

Chorus

Don Pannabecker of the business office
Works on his computer all day
And when we drop by, just to say "Hi"
He always continues to play.

Spoken:

Got PacMan figured out yet, Don?

Chorus

Arden Slotter is our dean you see
Has to be tutored to count to three
He calls me on the phone 'cause he's all alone
But Elmer refuses to let him go home.

Spoken:
You have to work until five, Dean.

Chorus

Then there's the president, who runs the show
He works from nine 'til three
And he says with a groan, as he answers his phone
You can buy it if it's free.
Spoken:
And, you have a purchase order. No, no, we have to take
that to committee.

Chorus

Old Harvey, he's in the know
He works in the library all day
But when he goes home, he won't answer his phone
'cause he's reading Playboy they say.
Spoken:
With the shades pulled.

Chorus

Well, I'm about done and it's been lots of fun
Singing this little ditty
But I'm sure you know, I really must go
'cause I'm looking for a job don't you see.
Spoken:
Anybody want to write me a recommendation? Forward
my mail, please.

Chorus

Mission accomplished! The spring prior to my singing of the above song at the fall faculty gathering, the Board of Trustees unanimously voted to award me tenure. I knew they couldn't fire me; or at least, I didn't think they could.

"King of the Old Gridiron"

At this same faculty retreat, the administrative staff came back with their own volley to my "The Administrative Staff, Plus One," and sang it to the faculty and guests. I wasn't aware that they knew beforehand of my composition, so it caught me by surprise. It is sung to the tune of "Ballad of Davy Crockett," and is titled "King of the Old Gridiron."

> *Came to Bluffton from Nelsonville*
> *Brought with him Sharon, and Kelly, and Jill*
> *Said he would win, win right away*

Spoken:
> *You pay attention, to what I say.*

Chorus:
> *Carlin, Carlin Carpenter*
> *King of the old gridiron.*

> *The first few years were awful grim*
> *The points were few and the crowds were slim*
> *A cloud of dust, two times up the middle*
> *Then fumble the ball and say, "Oh fiddle!"*

Spoken:
> *1979, 80, 81; wins 5, losses 21, ties 1.*

Chorus

> *The losses kept mounting, but Carlin hung in*
> *Diverted our attention with his wit and grin*

He'd share a few stories and pick his guitar
Spoken:
> *But no one ever took him for a country music star.*
> *1982, 1983, 1984; wins 5, losses 22, ties 0.*

Chorus

There's a story that Elmer called him in
Said your pickin' ain't cool and your team's gotta' win
Carlin ditched his guitar and revised his plan
Spoken:
> *And said, "I better become a football winnin' man."*

Chorus

Sure enough the drought did end
We won a few games; the team was on the mend
Carlin felt secure, the team was doing well
There was spring in his legs, and he was feeling swell.
Spoken:
> *The story about the race: 100 meter dash, Monday, August 22, 1983, 11:30 a.m.*

Chorus

Got so cocky that he challenged big Don
Said he could outrun him and the race was on
Halfway down the track, Don turned around
There was Carlin just startin' and still pawin' the ground.
Spoken:
> *Schweingruber 11.3 seconds. Carpenter 1 minute 17 seconds.*

Chorus

> *The last few years the team has been winnin'*
> *On that craggy old face there's lots of grinnin'*
> *The players are in place, the coaches are all picked*
> *Now it's up to Carlin to keep from gettin' licked.*

Spoken:

> *1985, 1986, 1987; wins 22, loses 6, ties 0.*

Chorus

> *After witnessin' his display*
> *One by one he critiqued away*
> *His little story about six plus one*
> *Has led to our delivering this stern ultimatum.*

> *Eight and one isn't enough*
> *There's no room for error, not even a muff*
> *The pressure is on, a championship we demand*

Spoken:

> *Carlin, if you lose just once, you're nothing but a guitar playin' man.*

> *Chorus, everyone!*

That fall, 1988, Beavers were undefeated. However, the last win didn't come until after the season, when it was revealed that Bill Ramseyer, Wilmington (OH) College's head coach, played an ineligible player. It was reported that the winning touchdown was caught by that player, although I have never been able to verify it.

We had the game won until Greg Gilcrease stepped out of bounds on a third-down play, stopping the clock. That was the closest I ever came to murdering someone. That caused us to punt, thus giving the Quakers time enough to score and take the lead with only a few seconds remaining in the game. Following the contest, I presented Bill and his team with the game ball. They deserved it. I was out-coached. Bill Ramseyer is a good man and coach.

"The Five-Pound Box of Cheese"

Whenever our budget would allow, my staff and I would attend the American Football Coaches Association (AFCA) annual convention. Usually our wives would also attend with us, but had to finance their own trip. Their organization was the American Football Coaches Wives Association (AFCWA) and would meet in conjunction with the AFCA.

As chairman of the Coach of the Year Committee, I received $500 from the AFCA each year to help defray the cost of my travel to the convention. I would split this money with the wives in order for them to afford to attend the clinic. The conventions were held all over the United States in a new location each year.

These clinics consisted of professional help sessions, award banquets, and social functions. One of the social functions was the Brown Derby Talent Contest. It featured coaches showcasing some talent unrelated to football. There were singers, musicians, comedians, ventriloquists, magicians, etc. who would participate. There were awards for the first three places, with first place receiving round-trip air fare for two to the next convention. My staff and their wives would often attend this function to be entertained, plus take advantage of the free hors d'oeuvres and beverages.

In 1998, the convention was held in Dallas, Texas, at the Hilton Anatole Hotel. As usual, we all attended. The auditorium, in which the Brown Derby event was held, seated around 1,000 guests and the place was full.

I had never participated as a contestant in the event, even though my ego wanted to show my singing skills. Sharon would always discourage me with, "Don't be stupid, you can't sing!"

As the show progressed, I was not impressed with the talent

and felt I could do better. The master of ceremonies was a friend of mine, so I approached him and requested permission to participate, even though I had not pre-registered. He granted my request, and I borrowed a twelve-string guitar from one of the contestants. When it was my turn, I proceeded to the stage. I was experiencing some stage fright in that I had never played a twelve-string before, and Sharon's criticism of my singing kept running through my mind.

My presentation was a story about my father becoming a veterinarian followed by a song titled "The Five-Pound Box of Cheese." I had performed the routine at one of the college's faculty retreats, and President Neufeld wasn't too impressed with it—too risqué!

"The Five-Pound Box of Cheese" Routine

My father worked for Sunday Creek Coal Company all his life. For the first twenty years, he worked underground and the last ten as a maintenance man in the yard. His maintenance tools consisted of a roll of duct tape, WD40, and a pair of pliers. If it moved and wasn't supposed to, he would tape it; if it didn't move and was supposed to, he would spray it with WD40. He never used his pliers.

Dad hated mine work, so one day, out of frustration, he arrived home and informed mom that he had quit the mine and was going to become a veterinarian.

Mom went bananas, "You can't be a vet, you don't have enough education!"

Dad claimed he had been around animals all his life and had enough education to do the job, claiming he had twenty years of schooling "I graduated from the tenth grade twice."

We had an old shed out back that we used as storage. Dad cleaned it out and painted "Veterinarian" on its side. I think it said veterinarian, or maybe vegetarian, I'm not sure. Neither dad nor I could read or spell very well.

Although dad was open for business, no one took advantage of his services, but that was about to change. There was an ole' mule, Clyde, at our high school who got sick. He was used to teach driver's education and sex ed, which was an important part of our curricula.

The principal had the mule treated by vets from town, but nothing seemed to work. Dad decided to give it a try. He and I went to the school and talked the principal into allowing dad to take the mule home for some TLC. Dad guaranteed he could have Clyde ready for action in one week. Dad pumped him full of castor oil and covered him with yogurt mixed with cow manure. In one week, Clyde was cured!

Dad's favorite treatment, his only treatment, was to force-feed any sick critter castor oil. He claimed that most just needed to be flushed out, after which they would recover, as did the mule.

After dad cured the mule word got around of his medical skills, and people started bringing their pets for dad to treat. Most were animals with minor problems, and the cleaning out did the trick. With positive reports from pet owners whose pets dad had cured, business flourished. Three of the most memorable cases involved a goat, a dog, and a chicken.

Ticky Coleman brought his pet goat, Hogan, to see dad, claiming the goat had eaten two pounds of un-popped popcorn. As normal, dad force-fed Hogan a quart of castor oil. Ticky was concerned that the popcorn might explode, so dad told him to keep Hogan out of the sun for a few days until the oil moved him.

Skillet Davis had an ugly basset hound that had swallowed a shotgun shell. Skillet feared the shell would discharge before he could get him to see dad, so Skillet had

Boso covered with bubble wrap and tethered to a thirty-yard leash; safety first. Treatment, castor oil! Skillet wanted to know if the shell would fire once the castor oil hit and dad responded, "I'm not sure, but to be safe, you better keep his rear aimed toward the woods."

Things were going really well the first few weeks of dad's new career, but things were about to turn sour.

Bod Pack's pet chicken was losing its feathers and he brought it to the clinic. As usual, dad gave him the normal treatment and agreed to keep the chicken for a few days to be sure it was cured. Disaster!

The Rock Island Red died. Dad, not wanting to disappoint Bob, stuffed it. Bob wasn't too happy about the situation but, after all, his chicken was returned.

The next day, we changed the sign on the shed to, "Veterinarian, Taxidermist…Either way, you get your pet back."

Word got around that dad's treatment had killed Bob's clucker and business fell off, to the point we had to go on welfare. When one goes on welfare, it entitles each member of one's family to a free five- pound box of government cheese. There were five in our family: mom, dad, grandma, me, and our dog Blaze. Mom questioned dad about including Blaze as a family member, but dad insisted that Blaze was as much a member as she was.

Every Thursday, I would take our wheelbarrow to the First Baptist Church and pick up our free cheese, twenty-five pounds—five pounds for each family member. The first week we had cheese omelets, cheese sandwiches, fried cheese, cheese kabobs, cheese and crackers, cheese soup, and a vast variety of other ways cheese can be prepared.

Things were good, but regardless of how much cheese we ate, by week's end, there were always twenty pounds left over. After a month, we had eighty pounds of cheese left over and stored in every corner of our house. Mice love cheese! We had mice migrating to our house from Mexico and Canada! Cats love mice! Every cat in the neighborhood took up residence under our front porch waiting for its next chubby meal.

Finally, mom had had enough and demanded, "Sell the cheese!"

This was going to be a problem, in that everybody we knew got free cheese. But dad agreed to sell the stuff, and set out to formulate a marketing plan. If we could come up with a slogan or jingle that would make people want to buy it, dad was convinced that the cheese could be sold.

After much searching for a gimmick to sell the cheese, we finally settled on a song that would promote sales. The song we chose is titled "The Five-Pound Box of Cheese," composed by acquaintance J. D. Jewell, a railroader from Athens County, Ohio. It goes like this:

Well, I got a little tax rebate
Oh, just the other day
The food stamps folks, they said to me
Come on down this way.

We have a little gift for you
At which you cannot sneeze
Please come by and pick up your
Five-pound box of cheese.

Well a job I've been search'n
For several months gone by
I just know'd them folks in Washington
Won't let me starve and die.

Under this administration
Just set back and take your ease

But I wish they'd serve some crackers
With this five-pound hunk of cheese.

Well I've cut down on the water bill
No toilets now to flush
I'm stopped up tighter than a drum
My face red like a blush.

No one has to holler
Do not squeeze the Charmin please
I don't need no toilet tissue
With this five-pound box of cheese.

I went out a-court'n
With my favorite girl last night
She took one look at me
And said pretty baby you ain't right.

Then she laid a kiss on me
And gave a mighty squeeze
And all at once out popped that whole
Five-pound box of cheese.

A messy situation
It was to say the least
That All-American pasteurized
Smelled like it was deceased.

I'll still take your food stamps
Refuel so I don't freeze
But I don't think I want another
Five-pound box of cheese.

I don't want any more
Of that bowel-binding cheese.

My presentation and song received resounding applause. Now it was time for the five judges to determine the winner. The winners were announced from third place to first. The third and second place winners were announced, and I wasn't one of them.

Then came the drum roll for the first and best performance: "And the winner of this year's Brown Derby Talent Contest is Carlin Carpenter of Bluffton College." My staff went nuts, including their wives, but Sharon sat in stunned silence.

I accepted the award of two round-trip plane tickets to next year's convention in Nashville, Tennessee, at the Grand Ole' Opry Hotel, and an invitation to perform there.

Over the years, I have performed "The Five-Pound Box of Cheese" routine from Bluffton, to Dallas, in Nashville, and at Jimmy Buffett's Margaritaville in New Orleans, Louisiana. For my efforts, I have been paid as much as $2,000 and as little as nothing for a performance. As expected, Sharon declared herself my agent and takes what money I earn.

In reality, my father, O. B. "Shine" Carpenter, managed a bulk liquid storage facility for petroleum and petroleum products for the Standard Oil Company of Ohio in Nelsonville and retired from that position after thirty years of service.

Dad succumbed to a massive stroke on March 2, 1975, the day I reported to Huntington, West Virginia, to start my new position as defensive coordinator of Marshall University's Thundering Herd. It was one of the most difficult transitions I have ever faced.

Animal Magnetism

Fridays were our most-attended recruiting days. Student-Athletes liked to visit on Fridays, in that it gave them a long weekend. On this particular Friday, we had 28 recruits plus parents. A good day!

The day started with a meeting with the group to explain our program, followed by a tour of campus, and then lunch. After lunch, I met with them to finalize their application process and Lawrence Matthews, our director of financial aid, would explain the forms.

Half-way through the closing session, one of my coaches entered the room proclaiming, "Your house is on fire!"

Immediately after, Sharon called, "Our house is on fire!"

By now, everyone in the room knew the situation. Wanting to show that the recruits were more important than my house, I informed Sharon, "When I finish here, I'll be home." That was a mistake!

When I finally arrived home, Sharon was standing in front of our house, crying, watching the firemen desperately trying to extinguish the fire. She was not happy with my decision, and thought I should have immediately gone home.

I tried a little humor to cool her off, "I have no experience in fighting fires. What did you expect me to do?" Another mistake!

All of our belongings were destroyed by fire or smoke, and the interior was a total loss. We contacted our insurance carrier and were given several hundred dollars to replace some of our wardrobe, plus a stipend to cover meals and lodging. Sharon, Jill, and I, along with Jill's cat, Tiki, moved to the L&K Motel in Bluffton, where we spent the next 94 days.

It was the worst 94 days of my life. We shared a single room with two double beds, one bathroom, one chair, one dresser, a TV, and we brought a litter box for TiKi. Being with Sharon and Jill was not the problem. It was TiKi! When Sharon and I were at work and Jill at school, TiKi would sleep. All day! Come night, she explored every corner of the room. Up on the dresser; jump to the chair, then to the bed, on the TV, back to the dresser, in the litter box, an endless carousel around the room. All night! Just when one would finally get to sleep, she would land on your head or some other body part. She was driving us crazy!

Kelly was a student at the college and would stay with us on some weekends and during the school's vacation periods. Kelly threatened to sleep in the car in order to get some relief from that damn cat.

I am not a cat lover. Tiki had to go! I informed Sharon that Tiki was about to use all nine of her lives, but Sharon wasn't too enthused about my plan; after all, it was Jill's cat. Sharon recommended, "Just put her out at night." I accepted the compromise, and did as instructed. This was my chance to get rid of Tiki. If I put her out at night, I knew she wouldn't return. Wrong! Every morning at daybreak, Tiki would be at the door. Guess who had to get up at dawn to let her in? I did not have one good night's sleep for 94 days.

Our house was finally restored, and Sharon, Kelly, Jill, and I returned home, along with TiKi. Later, Tiki passed away. Over the years, Jill has owned several cats; TuFu, Big Toe, Willie, and TiKi, but TiKi was the worst of all. That feline should have been called The Cat From Hell. I don't miss her.

Kelly graduated from Bluffton in 1986, and is presently the executive director of a retirement community in Perrysburg, Ohio. She is married to Dave Ebersbach, one of my former assistants, and they have one child, Bryce. Bryce is my middle name.

Jill is a 1996 Bluffton College graduate and is an intervention specialist, vocational special education coordinator, Findlay City Schools, Millstream Career Center, Findlay, Ohio. Jill has three children; Alexa, Carlin, and Kaley.

Rabbit Phobia

In 1987, the Beavers qualified for the NAIA National Playoffs for the first time in school history. The playoffs started in late November, and it was bitter cold; cold-cold. The ground was frozen, but we still had to prepare for Geneva College (Beaver Falls, PA). As players slowly walked to practice, it was evident that it was not going to be a good one. All were dressed as if they were going hunting in Alaska and were complaining about the weather.

After they all finally arrived, we started our warm-up routine. One exercise required the players to lie on the ground, which was frozen. They all started to complain about having to make contact with the frozen turf, but finally complied. As their backsides kept getting colder, they became increasingly cranky. I was slowly losing my patience.

A few yards beyond the edge of the practice field was a dead rabbit, frozen stiff. I slowly walked over, retrieved the rabbit, and busted Jesse Williams in the head with it. Of course, he was wearing his helmet, so no damage. He didn't know what I had hit him with, and laughingly said, "Is that all you got?" I then laid the rabbit on his chest. Jesse went ballistic! He had a phobia for rabbits and took off running, with me close behind swinging Peter Cottontail. The rest of the practice was outstanding.

As a result of a goal line fumble late in the game, we lost to Geneva, but defeated Cumberland College (Williamsburg, KY) in 1988, for the first playoff victory ever by the BC Beavers.

"I Miss My Pussy"

Offensive line play is the most demanding of all positions. It normally takes a few years for one to master it, but one young player in the mid '90s was making steady progress and was playing often in a backup role. We were having a good season, and he was playing well enough to start our next game.

On Tuesday, he came into my office and stated he had to go home. Over the years, many players have had to deal with an emergency at home, so this was not an unusual situation. Normally, they would go home, address the problem, and return in a day or two. I always stressed the importance of God, family, academics, and football in that order, so one was expected to deal with any family crises that might arise over football.

Selfishly, concerned that I might lose a starting offensive lineman, I inquired when he would return. To my surprise, he responded, "I'm not coming back."

Leaving school was common for those who could not deal with being away from home because they were suffering from separation anxiety, more commonly known as homesickness. None would admit to being homesick, so I have heard every excuse imaginable for leaving: bed too hard, can't sleep; bed too soft, can't sleep; food no good, losing weight; food too good, gaining weight; roommate not friendly, roommate too friendly; etc. But upperclassmen hardly ever left as a result of being homesick.

My first response as to his impending departure was, "Why?"

"I miss my pussy."

"Whoa!" This seemed like a crude way to refer to one's girlfriend, but I continued to question him about his decision for leaving. "How long has she been your girlfriend?"

"About three years."

"Does she ever come to campus to visit?"

"Yes, mom brings her to all of our home games."

Knowing that he lived within a short drive from Bluffton, I asked, "Do you ever go home to see her during the week?"

"Yes, about every week; plus, I go home on the weekends after the home games."

This sounded like a serious love affair, so I pressed for more details. "Are you so serious about your relationship with your girlfriend that you are willing to forfeit your opportunity to get an education?"

"Yeah, Coach, I really love her."

I had to come up with a plan to keep him in school, thus keeping him as one of my starting offensive lineman. On one occasion, a player got married during the summer. I got his wife a job in Bluffton, and he remained in school and on the team. If I could get them to the altar, problem solved!

Thinking I had a solution to the problem, I asked, "In that she has been your girlfriend for three years, I presume you both are in love?"

"Yes sir, we love each other."

"If that is the case, have you thought about marriage?"

"Marriage? You can't marry a cat!"

"Are you telling me your girlfriend is a cat?"

"Yeah, Coach. I love that cat."

I verbally conveyed the first thing that came to my mind, "You gotta' be shittin' me!"

He wasn't and I haven't seen or heard from him since.

Caesar, The Wrestling Bear

I read in the local paper that an event was going to take place at the American Legion in Columbus Grove, Ohio, concerning a wrestling bear. It was advertised as "Caesar, the wrestling bear, will take on all comers." This sounded interesting. Was Caesar a bear of a man, or was Caesar a bear-bear? I called a friend, Terry Callahan, proprietor of Miller's Lunch in Grove, to check. Caesar was a bear-bear.

This I had to see! I contacted Louie Stokes, one of my assistants, and he agreed to attend the event with me. The place was sold out and Caesar made short work of every opponent. After the event, I talked with Caesar's handler and asked what he charged to bring his bear to the event.

The price sounded reasonable. Founders could seat approximately 1500, including the stage. At $3 per person, plus concessions, this could be a great way to raise funds for the football program. I later contacted the handler and booked Caesar.

We agreed on a date, and now all I had to do was get some challengers. In order to make it interesting and profitable, I knew the challengers had to be well known on the campus and in the community. I volunteered to be one and canvased for others. Bluffton's mayor, Roger Edwards, and Alison Thompson, a volleyball player, agreed; plus, Ray Ruggley, a local citizen, and Dr. J. Denny Weaver, professor of religion, were in. I volunteered some of my players to fill the remaining five positions, for a total of 10 challengers.

The big night arrived! A few minutes prior to the event, Caesar's handler met with all of the contestants to prep them for the event, "No poking him in the eyes, do not pull on his ears, and by all means, don't hit him in his privates. Doing so will make him go crazy!"

J. Denny had a question, "If one would accidently hit Caesar below the waist, what would happen?"

"Two weeks ago that happened, and he bit the guy's ear off." Denny turned pale and became quite restless. At one point, I thought he might withdraw as a challenger.

I turned to Denny and assured him that the trainer was kidding. Dr. Weaver believed me and agreed to participate in the event.

Following the prep session, we all lined up in Founders Hall waiting to be introduced. Each person was dressed in a costume and led into the auditorium with an entourage. Mayor Edwards wore a judge's robe and carried a gavel, there was a cowboy, and one wrestler wore a Superman's cape. I wore a tutu over long underwear and hunting boots. As each wrestler was introduced, a spotlight illuminated their entry. The announcer, "And now entering, World Wrestling Federation champion, "Bone Crusher Edwards." The crowd went crazy!

After all the challengers were introduced, it was time for Caesar to make his entrance. The crowd gasped when this black, hairy mass bounded in. He was big! No muzzle, and with all his claws! The only thing I could think of was, *I hope he's not hungry!*

What had I gotten myself into? As the event progressed, it was evident no one was going to put Caesar on his back; however, Alison Thompson came the closest of all.

Caesar slapped us around like rag dolls, but no one was seriously injured, including the bear. We netted over $3,000, and the People for the Ethical Treatment of Animals (PETA) were happy that we didn't hurt the bear. There wasn't any chance of us injuring him.

A few years later, I read in the *Lima News* that Caesar had attacked and killed his trainer. He must have hit Caesar in his privates. I sent the article to J. Denny Weaver, who had retired and relocated to Wisconsin. Knowing Denny, he probably didn't sleep a wink for a couple of weeks.

On a side note, my assistant Louie met his future wife, Melanie Taylor, at the Legion bear wrestling. I think she liked me better, but I was already married.

Player Ailments

Vance Nofziger was a starting defensive back and kick returner from Archbold, Ohio, and he had asthma. Heat, dust, pollen, and fatigue do not go well with asthma, but that didn't stop Vance. One can only imagine not being able to breath, especially playing a game that requires maximum oxygen intake.

Many times during practices and games, Vance would have to use his atomizer to continue, but he insisted on continuing to participate. He would take a shot from his atomizer and go back in action. What strength! His drive and determination exceeded those with no hypoxia.

After the first few attacks during a game, his asthma became somewhat of an asset. Whenever he had an attack, we would get a free timeout. When things weren't going well on the field, an attack would follow, which resulted in an uncharged timeout. Of course, feigning an injury is a violation of the rules. I never questioned Vance's integrity, because many times those uncharged timeouts came in handy, especially if we were out of our three charged ones per half. To this day, he swears all of his attacks during the game were legit. Historically, Archbold is described as a Christian community in Fulton County, so who wouldn't believe a citizen from there?

I see Vance often, and our paths crossed last year in the parking lot adjacent to Burcky Gym. He extended his hand for me to shake and I said, "I don't want to shake your hand Vance. I need a big hug." I hugged him and planted a kiss on his cheek, saying "I love you Vance! You are the greatest!" A few months later, he informed me that he had been having the worst day of his life, and my greeting changed his state of mind.

I greet most of my former players with a hug and a kiss on the cheek, which they return. Every person you meet is dealing with some burden unknown to you, and a kind word or gesture may mean more than one realizes.

Early in his career, Vance played running back for the Beavers and earned honorable mention in the Association of Mideast Colleges in 1992. As a defensive back his senior year, Vance earned 1994 first team AMC honors.

The Exam

Speed is the most disruptive force in any sport, and Lamarr Renshaw ran a 4.40 forty-yard dash, pro speed. He was 5' 10", 174 pounds, and played his high school career as quarterback at Trotwood-Madison High School (Trotwood, OH).

The first time I saw Lamarr on film, I wanted him at Bluffton and aggressively started the recruiting process. Unfortunately, he chose Kentucky State University (Frankfort, KY). But I refused to give up on him. He left KSU during fall practice and had not registered for classes. Good news for me! I called him and he decided to give Bluffton a try.

Lamarr had a rough first year. He started as our quarterback but didn't have the passing skills to continue at that position, so we moved him to wide receiver. He showed great promise at receiver, but was not particularly happy with the move and transferred to Eastern Michigan University (Ypsilanti, MI).

Even though he had transferred, I often called his mother to inquire about his welfare. On several occasions, she commented, "Lamarr is not at peace with himself." Translated, I took this to mean he wasn't happy at Eastern Michigan, so I kept calling mom. One day, much to my surprise, he called and wanted to return to Bluffton. He was willing to play receiver as opposed to quarterback. Lamarr adjusted to playing a wide-out like a duck to water.

During his junior year we were scheduled to play at Mount St. Joseph College of Cincinnati at a stadium near Kings Island Resort, Mason, Ohio. The week prior to the game, Lamarr was not having a particularly good week of practice. He was not running his pass routes properly, and I was on his case most of each practice. His excuse was, "My back hurts!" Of course, I had Phill Talavinia, our trainer, examine him. No problem was detected.

About an hour before the kickoff on game day, he informed me that his mother wanted him to drink cranberry juice because she thought it would help his back. I was at my wit's end and decided to get some of Mom's prescribed juice in hopes it would work like spinach on Popeye. I sent a manger to the stands to tell Sharon what I needed and would she go get it? The manager returned and said Sharon wasn't too happy about the request, but agreed to try and find the "magic juice."

Sharon returned with a quart of cranberry juice, but she was not in the best of moods. She had a difficult time finding it. It was about five minutes before kickoff, and I took Lamarr out of warm-ups and summoned him to the sideline. "Here is your cranberry juice, now drink every damn bit of it!" He did.

Lamarr's effort and performance during the game weren't his standard play. He dropped several passes, one that would have been a touchdown. We lost 14-3.

Several times during the game Lamarr had to return to the

locker room to urinate. The cranberry juice didn't rally his football performance, but it did improve his kidney function.

The following week, he started complaining again. I had heard enough. I grabbed him by the arm, led him off the field to my car, and with ire said, "Get in!"

"Where are we going?"

"To the doctor," I replied.

"Can I change out of my uniform?"

"No! Take off your helmet and get in. Leave on the rest of your gear." Lamarr did as instructed and we headed to the office of Dr. Mark Steinmetz, our team physician.

Whenever we needed to take a player to see Dr. Steinmetz, an appointment was not necessary. We went to the back entrance, knocked, and Lamarr and I were escorted to an examining room.

Dr. Steinmetz entered and asked the usual questions associated with back pain. Then he ordered Lamarr to drop his pants and bend over the examining table. Oh boy, I knew what was about to take place, and I was waiting in joyful anticipation of Doc's next move.

I was seated directly across from Lamarr on the other side of the table. My face was about two feet from his, and I engaged him in idle conversation while Dr. Steinmetz prepared for the examination. Lamarr, curious as to what was about to happen, asked, "What is he going to do?"

I replied, "Check your prostate."

Lamarr didn't have any idea what a prostate was or where it was located, but he was about to find out. Finally, Dr. Steinmetz snapped on a rubber glove and applied a dab of petroleum jelly to his index finger. Lamarr glanced behind, then turned to me and repeated, "What is he going to do?"

"Nothing, relax!"

"Is he going to do something to my buuuuuuuutt!?"

Too late! With eyes big as saucers, Lamarr executed a vertical takeoff and landed on both knees in the middle of the examining table. Lamarr now knows where his prostate is located.

I called him a big baby as a result of his reaction to the exam, and the name stuck. From that day forth, I called him Baby Lamarr and he countered by referring to me as Big Daddy Carp.

Not once did he ever again complain about his back. Lamarr came to peace with himself and developed into a premier receiver. At our Homecoming game against Sue Bennett College (London, KY), he returned a kickoff for a touchdown, a punt for a touchdown, and caught a pass for a touchdown. For his stellar performance, he was awarded NCAA, Division III, National Player of the Week.

Lamarr graduated in 1998 with a degree in business administration. He was selected by his peers to give the Baccalaureate address on graduation weekend. Lamarr and Chiem had their marriage ceremony performed at a botanical garden in Columbus, Ohio. Sharon and I celebrated the occasion with them. They have two children, Nia and Kenzie. Presently, he is employed by CenturyLink, and the Renshaws reside in Lewis Center, Ohio.

Lamarr was a joy to coach. I'm a better person for having known him.

Divine Intervention

The Beavers opened the 1992 season with a night game at Ohio Northern University. ONU had a strong team and we were young, so it was going to be interesting to see how our players would respond to such formidable opponents.

Things didn't start out too well. We fell behind early, and were playing catch-up without much success. Our offense was struggling, but our defense was holding its own. We had a good core of linebackers making some plays. Bob Bame, a junior from Dola, Ohio, was one of our backers, and was playing well.

Just before the half, Bob went down. Unless a player is down for an extended period of time, I usually didn't go on the field; injuries are part of the game. We had an excellent training staff, and they would attend to the injured. Besides watching, I served no useful medical purpose during these situations.

I typically used the uncharged timeout to make adjustments, but after a few minutes of doing so, I was surprised to see that Bob was still flat on his back. Normally, an injured player was up and coming to the sideline by the time I had finished talking to the unit. Bob had not moved.

Whenever a player is injured, the opposing team's trainer also goes on the field as a standby in case the attending medical staff needs assistance. Ohio Northern's trainer, Owen Keller, came out. Owen had no sooner gotten to Bob when he motioned to his sideline. That only meant one thing; he was summoning his team physician, as requested by our trainer. I went on the field and arrived at Bob's side the same time as Dr. Roger Terry, ONU's orthopedist. It is customary for the home team to provide a physician and an EMS unit.

Bob was unconscious. Dr. Terry spent a few seconds observing Bob and then motioned for the EMS ambulance, which was parked behind the end zone.

When Dr. Terry stood, I pulled him aside. "Is he going to be OK?"

"I don't think he will make it to the hospital. I'm going to ride in the ambulance with him."

"What do you mean?"

"He has a life threatening concussion, and I don't think he is going to make it!"

"You mean, like die?!"

"Yes."

Never in my 35 years of college coaching have I ever been confronted with such a tragic situation. I have dealt with sprains, breaks, and dislocations, but nothing like this. A wave of anxiety, fear, helplessness, and sadness swept over me.

There were only a few seconds left in the half, and when it ended, we went to the visiting team locker room.

The players did not know the seriousness of the situation, so I explained. The game was no longer of any importance. We all knelt and started praying through tears. We continued to pray until the official came with the two-minute warning.

Immediately following the game, I went to Memorial Hospital in Lima. Bob had regained consciousness, but was not aware of his surroundings. His parents and I remained with him most of the night.

When I returned Sunday evening, Bob was sitting up and alert. As a matter of fact, he was laughing. Our prayers had been answered.

Bob was released within the week and insisted on continuing his football career the next year. His parents approved, and he was cleared to resume contact for the 1993 season. Bob finished his junior and senior years as one of our top linebackers. He suffered no aftereffects from his injury.

We lost the game, but won our teammate's life. The power of prayer!

Bob was selected as a First Team AMC linebacker in his senior year.

Community Support

Over the years, I have had some outstanding part-time assistant coaches. Part-time meant they had a full-time job outside of the college and football team. By no means did "part-time" reflect the amount of hours they spent in meetings and on the field coaching.

Everett Collier juggled a full-time job as an employee with the United States Postal Service and his assistant coaching duties at Bluffton. Everett had had an exemplary career as a player at Bluffton College, earning first team Hoosier Buckeye Collegiate Conference (HBCC) and NAIA District 22 honors twice. In addition, he served as captain of the football team his senior year and was selected to play in the All Ohio Shrine Bowl at Ohio State stadium following his last year. We were happy to have him as a member of the staff.

Being a member of my staff required many long hours in meetings. During the season, meetings were held every day of the week except Fridays. During these meetings, the staff formulated the week's game plan, practice organization, recruiting procedures, and other policies to ensure the program ran smoothly.

In these meetings, many intense arguments occurred. Some I initiated just for the sake of arguing. At the onset of being a member of my staff, it was made clear that one's ego had to be checked at the door, or resentment would result from the arguments. If an argument reflected a mistake made in the past, the offending party was quickly reminded of his past error. The only method of winning an argument that was considered off limits was making a derogatory remark about one's family; otherwise, everything else was on the table. Once the staff meeting was adjourned, the argument was over and an amicable work atmosphere resumed.

Everett had a quick wit and remembered all the mistakes I had made in the past and used them to win many arguments between us. At the conclusion of the 1988 season, he left my staff to devote all his time to the local post office. Knowing that he couldn't get even in a staff meeting, I took one last shot at him by submitting an article to the *Bluffton News* titled "Give us Back Our Heroes,"which follows.

"Give Us Back Our Heroes" by Carlin B. Carpenter

Yesterday, as my wife and I were returning from a late breakfast at one of our local restaurants, a sighting of Everett Collier wearing a pair of short longs (or long shorts), emerged from an unconventional vehicle parked on the wrong side of the street. Being a friend of Everett, I stopped to inquire about this unusual scene. He was quick to inform me that he was not parked on the wrong side, the steering wheel was on the wrong side, and his britches were Bermuda shorts with knee stockings. At that point, I became painfully aware that the profound esteem, bordering on hero worship, that I had for the nation's postmen was shattered beyond repair.

Since childhood, I have idolized the postmen, whose equal rivaled the likes of Wyatt Earp, Buffalo Bill Cody and Roy

Rogers all rolled into one. I can still envision the postmen of the Pony Express braving the elements, not to mention robbers, snakes, and beasts, too awful to mention, on their mission to deliver the mail. Not rain, mud, nor snow, blood or hail stopped the mail. Now, if an inch of snow covers your walk, you are a prime candidate for a poison-pen letter, "Remove the snow, or no more mail!" Finally, after a few days of no mail, and Mother Nature refusing to come to your rescue, you clear the walk, only to discover that Everett will cut through three feet of snow in your front yard in order to save a few steps to the adjacent house.

During my developmental years, we had no walks, yet it did not deter the dedicated postal employees from delivering our mail. As a matter of fact, the absence of sidewalks was really only a minor inconvenience. Most of the time, our trusted carriers had to fend off the four or five dogs that sought refuge under our front porch from the noonday heat. They victoriously fought them off with the grace and cunning of Crocodile Dundee, after which they cheerfully dropped the mail in the milk can. No Mace either, just their bare hands and quick wit.

And the cost! Give me a break! Comparatively speaking, for what it costs weight-wise to send a letter to California (29 cents an ounce then, 45 cents now), I can fly commercially my 183 pound frame to California and return, plus still have enough left to take my football team to the Shannon on dollar night, and buy Everett two pairs of long pants or one pair of long pants and a shirt.

So come on Everett, give us back our heroes! Get rid of those funny trucks with the steering wheels on the wrong side, bring back those BIG postal bags in which one person could carry enough mail to service a community of 5,000, cinch up those long cotton Dickies work pants, pull on those four-buckle Arctics, and tote that mail with the pride and resolve reminis-

cent of your forbearers. Pee Wee Herman is finished! Our kids need real heroes! Don't let them down!

Everett still hasn't come up with a convincing rebuttal to my letter; however, he did present some damaging information about me during his speech at the recognition gathering for my retirement in Yoder Recital Hall. I thanked him for his not-so-kind remarks and followed by saying, "Everett, you are a suppository of information."

After serving thirty years with the USPS, sixteen of those as postmaster, Everett retired in 2011. I still see him often and value his friendship.

Camera Man

Mr. Vince Koza, long-time sports director of WLIO television in Lima, Ohio, would always visit our two-a-day practices and tape an interview with me, as well as shoot some staged action footage of our best players. Vince is a great broadcaster, and I can still hear him describing a breakaway run: "He could…go…all…the…way! Touchdown!"

In order not to interrupt the flow of our routine, he would arrive a few minutes prior to the start of practice; however, one day he came late. He knew that I was a stickler for punctuality, so he gave me his best excuse. Regardless of any excuse, whenever a player was late for a meeting or practice, it cost him four laps, which was approximately one mile. I exercised my right as the head coach to relegate Vince's punishment—one lap. He took his punishment in stride, and started to run. "Run" may not be the appropriate term; he did start out running, but ended in a slow walk.

All the time he was abiding by his punishment, his cameraman was taping it. When Vince arrived at work the next day, the sports staff had put music to his jaunt: the theme song from the movie *Chariots of Fire*.

Mr. Koza worked for WLIO from 1980 to 2008. On occasion, he writes an article for the *Lima News,* plus I often hear him on the radio. I always claimed that he had a face for radio. Vince always shot what I thought was my best side, but he claimed my best side was from the behind.

A Trip to the Veterinarian

Whenever possible, I would take a faculty or staff member to a home visit. Many times, it was their input that would convince a player and his family that Bluffton was the place to continue the recruit's education and play football. On one such occasion, I took Lawrence Matthews, our director of financial aid, to visit with Domont Watkins and his family. Domont was a graduate of Lima Senior High School. As usual, Lawrence did a bang-up job, and Domont later committed to 3C.

After each visit, I would offer to buy dinner, at a restaurant of their choice, for the faculty or staff member who accompanied me. Even though this visit was in Lima, I felt it was necessary to make the offer to Lawrence. He accepted and chose the Flying J truck stop and restaurant. Since he could have chosen any place, I thought his selection was a little unusual. After all, this was not an establishment known for its gourmet food, but did serve large portions for truckers' appetites. Lawrence's stature did not indicate he consumed much food.

That assumption turned out to be totally erroneous. For starters, he had a large orange juice and a tall glass of whole milk, followed by several trips to the buffet from which he ate enough biscuits and gravy to feed a family of five. Lawrence finished with a piece of pie and coffee. I ordered one egg over easy with white toast and a cup of coffee.

I couldn't believe that a man his size could eat so much! Since I doubted he would make it home with that much food in his stomach, I offered to stop at the nearest veterinarian's office to inquire if the vet could issue him a temporary permit to defecate in the street.

Lawrence is still the director of financial aid and does outstanding work. Many times, his financial aid presentation resulted in a recruit's committing to Bluffton.

I see Lawrence and his wife, Louise, in church every Sunday, and he still hasn't gained any weight. I'm convinced he has the metabolism of a lemming.

As for Lawrence's recruit, Domont led the team in tackles, which was the first time a defensive tackle had ever done so. He was a great one. Thanks to Lawrence, he chose Bluffton to continue his education and play football for the Beavers.

Irate Coaches

On the first day of fall practice, we would test the players to check the state of their physical condition. Each was supposed to follow a summer program, which we sent to them in early June. If they had followed it religiously, the test results would reveal their dedication. One of the cardiovascular tests was to time them in the mile run. In order to pass the test, running backs, receivers, and defensive backs had to clock a time of 6 minutes or less; linebackers and tight ends, 6 minutes and 15 seconds; and the offensive linemen and defensive linemen, 6:30.

Shortly after sending the summer workout to the players, I decided to shake things up. Why not have all personnel associated with the team tested for the status of their conditioning? This included student trainers and managers, plus my coaching staff.

I sent a notice to all involved that they would be tested, with a 7-minute mile as the benchmark. Being young, I knew the trainers and managers could make the time with ease, but not the coaches; however, I had no intention of testing my assistants. Even though I wasn't going to time my coaches, I thought it would be interesting to see how they would respond to the news that they would also be tested.

I didn't hear anything from the trainers and managers, but the coaches went bonkers. I loved it! Any time my assistants had an opportunity to "pull my chain," they did not hesitate to do so. Now I had them! Regardless of how much they protested, I kept reminding them that their cardiovascular condition was as important as our players. They knew I was right, but didn't think testing them was appropriate in the presence of the team. I stuck to my conviction!

For the next three months, my assistants worked out. Every time we played golf, I would inquire, "How's your workout going?" They would respond with a barrage of expletives and vowed to get even with me if it took the rest of their lives.

On the day of the testing, all of the trainers and managers passed with a 7-minute run or less. It was time for the coaches to be tested. Prior to the run, I had them all stretch and walk a lap, explaining, "I don't want you to pull anything that would keep you out of practice. When you finish your walk, the testing will begin." They spent an exorbitant amount of time warming up. It was if they were delaying a trip to the gas chamber.

I lined them all on the starting line. "On your mark, get set, report to the staff room for further instructions." They chased me to the office, happy that they didn't have to run, but threatened, "If you ever do anything like that again, we will kill you!"

Over the years, I have had an outstanding staff. Any success we have had, I owe to them.

In the Offseason

I always looked forward to summers because they allowed me to do two activities I enjoy most: fishing and golfing. The day after graduation, I loaded my 10-foot jon boat, electric motor, battery, two rods, tackle box, and golf clubs into my station wagon, and they stayed there most of the summer, ready for quick access. Whenever I passed a lake or golf course I liked, out they came.

Shortly after the last term ended prior to summer vacation, Ms. Linda Suter, our registrar, called and requested that I offer a course for two first-time international students from Nigeria. Both had arrived early to get acclimated to being away from home. She informed me they were going to enroll full-time come fall, but needed some exposure to college work prior to classes beginning in late August.

I agreed and chose to offer golf. Admittedly, this may not have been the optimum course to expose them to the rigors of college academics, but it would serve the purpose. I reasoned it would get me on the golf course and provide them with college credit.

The first day we were to meet, I received a call from one of them, asking, "Can you give us a ride to the golf field?"

Obviously, teaching them golf was going to be a challenge. As we were driving to the Bluffton "golf field," one wanted to know if I had "sticks" they could use. Now, I really had my doubts if golf was a good choice to teach as a first-time exposure to college academia.

When we arrived at the course, I took them to the first tee and explained that there are 18 tees, followed by 18 fairways, and 18 greens, with each green containing a hole in which one was to put the ball. I explained the handicap system and how it allowed all golfers to compete on an even basis, regardless of their skill.

The first question, "Are handicapped people allowed to use wheelchairs?"

This is going to be a real challenge.

Trying to explain golf and the rules to a person who has no idea about the game is, at best, difficult. It's like trying to explain an elephant to a sightless person. Thinking they could get a better understanding of the game, I decided to play through a few holes while they followed and observed. I told them to get the gear out of the station wagon, while I checked in at the club house.

When I returned, on the first tee were my golf clubs, along with my boat, electric motor, battery, two rods, and they were headed back to the car to get my tackle box. Not surprised, a crowd of golfers had gathered to see what was going to transpire.

For the next year, whenever I went to the Bluffton course, someone would remind me of the safari.

"How's the fishing on number 5?"

"Bob said they are biting on 12." The comments always were followed with a round of laughter by all, including me.

The two young men from Nigeria did learn to play golf, one quite well. I enjoyed working with them.

***

Winter Formal Storm

My top priority as head football coach was to make certain that all those who participated in the program graduated. This was beneficial to our program, the student-athletes, and their parents: senior-dominated teams are most times successful, the player would be prepared to enter the work force, and parents would realize a return on their investment.

The biggest obstacle to this goal was how the player conducted himself off the field. Nothing we did in football would jeopardize the probability of earning a degree; however, a player's poor conduct as it related to the campus community *could* jeopardize a degree, and severely. A large portion of my time was spent putting out fires resulting from unacceptable social behavior.

One of the many social problems with which I had to deal occurred at the 1999 Winter Formal. This was an all-campus dance with a DJ. The day following the dance, I was informed by Dr. Don Schweingruber, Dean of Student Affairs, that four of my players' behavior at the Formal was inappropriate, so I chose to call each to my office to address the situation. The following public response, by one of those with whom I met, appeared as a Letter to the Editor in the campus newspaper, *The Witmarsum*, Friday, February 12, 1999:

Calling All Beavers,

Recently, I was disciplined for my actions at the Winter Formal. I was told that my involvement of using profanity towards the DJ's choice of music did not conform to the Bluffton College "Community of Respect" philosophy. I have come to terms with the way in which I was disciplined (by the dean of student affairs). However, while sitting in a member of our faculty's office, I was hit with a barrage of explicit and rude phrases, the likes of such were far worse than any language I ever used at the dance. Such name calling included "a**hole", *"dumba**", and "stupid mother**er." I was asked if I must be "institutionalized," and upon asking to see a rule book, I was told that I was "probably too f**ing stupid to read anyway." After which I promptly left the office.*

I can take criticism but how can anyone sit behind a desk and scold me in this manner and it not be considered violating the "Community of Respect?" It is hypocritical, what could I possibly learn from this? Swearing is what I got in trouble for in the first place and this is how I am reprimanded: by graphic name calling? I ask you Bluffton College, how can this "Community of Respect" be taken seriously when members of the core of the institution, the faculty, do not adhere to it?

Signed,
BC Junior

Panic mode! I was sure President Lee Snyder more than likely had read this in *The Witmarsum.* If she hadn't, Dr. Schweingruber knew of the situation and would be obligated to inform her if she asked about it. He knew I intended to call each player to my office.

My defense follows in the letter I drafted and hand-delivered to President Snyder's secretary, Sue Hardwick:

February 15, 1999
Dear President Snyder:

Last week's Witmarsum "Calling All Beavers" letter to the editor caught me by surprise in that it was a private conversation, in my office, between a football player and me. Actually, there were four players with whom I met privately, and discussed their behavior at the Winter Formal, plus past events in which they have been involved.

This type of behavior by these four has been ongoing for the past three years. It has involved, among other things: miss-

ing class, throwing food in the cafeteria, numerous alcohol re-ferrals, criminal alcohol related charges which have included public intoxication, resisting arrest, threatening a police officer, threatening a police officer's family via phone message (it was traced to his room), plus a telephone death threat to one of our minority students, telephone sexual harassment of one of our coeds, numerous physical and verbal altercations on campus, not complying with sanctions imposed by our campus judicial system, and the last incident, use of profanity toward the disc jockey at the dance. These are only a few. There are others of which I'm aware, some I can verify, some I can't.

Collectively, these four players have been in my office more than anybody else, each time one-on-one. My discussions with them have always been a civil exchange in which they acknowl-edged their unacceptable behavior, agreed to a punishment in lieu of being dismissed from the team, and promised to never be involved in less than noble behavior ever again. In an attempt to insure that they understood that I am condemning their be-havior and not them personally, I usually end the meeting with a hug and verbal affirmation of my confidence in them.

As a consequence of their inappropriate behavior, and in an attempt to try and deter it, I have met countless times with them one-on-one, had other team members talk with them, they have been sanctioned by our judicial system, I have involved them in community service projects, plus called and/or written their parents on numerous occasions to seek counsel or inform them of past events, but nothing seems to alter their actions.

After the incident at the Winter Formal, I felt it was time to change my approach and give them the same treatment to which they have been routinely subjecting others. I did it in the privacy of my office, each separately. Although you may find this type of exchange unorthodox, I felt it was appropriate for the situation; however, I am profoundly sorry that it left the readers speculating that it could be any member of our faculty. The dedication and professionalism of our faculty is beyond reproach, and I would never do anything to intentionally tarnish that. I'm not aware of what is appropriate journalism, but it seems to me that with minimum investigative work, the editor could have identified me as the faculty member in question and noted it some place. I'm disappointed that he/she allowed our faculty to be exposed to this type of suspicion.

In hindsight, at some point, I probably should have suspended all of them from the team, or at least chosen another method in an attempt to change their behavior. Although this may sound trite, I consider every player in my charge to be a family member. I've never counseled any of them to do anything that was not in their best interest. I expend a great deal of energy trying to keep them in school, because if they stay, graduation is almost certain. Over the last twenty years, I can only recall four players who stayed four years in our program who did not receive their diplomas. Three of these have since earned their degrees.

Even the writing of an anonymous letter is not in keeping with what I preach. I've always encouraged them to stand up for what they believe. Don't ever take the nameless, faceless anonymity route waiting for support from others. You may have to stand alone.

I take full responsibility for my behavior.

Sincerely,
Carlin B. Carpenter
Director of Athletics
Head Football Coach

I didn't hear anything back from President Snyder. The only thing left was to make an appointment to see her and be prepared to take my medicine, as bitter as it might be. I scheduled a meeting.

As I recall, whenever President Snyder wanted to reprimand me, she always sat behind her desk. Today, she joined me in the adjacent chair in her office, a good sign! She had my letter in her hand and asked what it was about. She hadn't read the article in *The Witmarsum*! With the style and grace of a Philadelphia lawyer, I explained the situation.

A few days later, I received a letter from President Snyder in response to the situation.

February 17, 1999
Dear Carlin:

I want to thank you for your letter of February 15 responding to an accusatory student letter in a recent Witmarsum. Understandably, the development in this case with a football player who was being disciplined has taken us aback in its criticism of faculty.

Your explanation of personal involvement in this situation provides helpful background. I appreciate your statement that you are responsible for your behavior in this incident, and I expect that this will not happen again. We shall go on from here.

I know you work extremely hard with students in difficulty: whether that is in area of discipline for inappropriate behavior or in academics. Many credit their success to a great extent to you.

With your permission, I have shared your letter with the two deans. We shall learn what we can through this and continue to work with students on fostering a healthy community of respect.

Sincerely,
Lee Snyder
President

No further action was taken.

After two years, I received a hand written letter from one of the four involved in the Winter Formal incident.

1/15/01

Coach Carpenter,

Congratulations on the outstanding season. Everyone seems really excited, especially about getting a ring.

I'm writing to thank you for allowing me to use you as a reference and for always keeping me in line when I was at Bluffton. For a long time, I thought you were the most evil S.O.B. on earth. Now, I realize sometimes you have to be put on your ass before you can learn to stand, THANKS. Beaver Football was the best thing that could have happened to me. Thanks for the chance and the memories.

Jarret
P.S. It's no gas station!

The reference to a gas station is the result of me telling Jarret Smotrila, on numerous occasions, "If you don't get your act together, you will spend the rest of your life in greasy overalls pumping gas."

Jarret had an outstanding career as a defensive back. Jarret still holds the school record for career interception yardage at 284 and twice earned post-season award honors in the HCAC. He was also All-America Honorable Mention. He graduated and is Vice President/COO of Merchant Cooperative, Goose Creek, South Carolina. Because of his intelligence and caring parents, I secretly felt he would make it and conveyed my thoughts in a congratulatory letter.

The other three involved in the Winter Formal Storm all graduated and are highly successful professionals.

I have played in the annual Bluffton Golf Outing with most of them, and we blame each other in jovial banter as to who was at fault; however, we all agree that the situation could have been handled differently.

I never did identify who wrote the letter to *The Witmarsum,* and it really doesn't matter. Legendary coach A.C. Burcky once told me, "When one uses profanity, it is usually the result of a depleted vocabulary."

How true!

Accepting Criticism

Recruiting is the foundation of any successful program. It is always work, but a few years before my retirement, it was becoming even more difficult. My competitors would always bring up the fact that I was nearing retirement and there was a good chance I would not be around to see their son through four years of football. I would always respond, "I have a lifetime contract and plan to be around for a long time."

I did have tenure, but I wasn't sure of its terms. A lifetime contract sounded good though, and usually ended the speculation. On occasion, a bold parent would ask my age. I would jokingly respond, "How old do you want me to be? Age is mind over matter. If you don't mind, it don't matter." That would usually bring a chuckle and we would move on.

But in reality, I was coming to the end of my coaching career, and the rigors of the job were beginning to show, especially in my hair. It was becoming increasingly grayer. I have always had the face of a 70-year old, but my body looked pretty good, if I do say so myself. Solution, dye my hair.

Lynda Best, a local beautician who is the proprietor of the Village Cut and Curl, had cut my hair since my arrival in Bluffton. She originally worked out of a house across from the Family Dollar Store, but later moved to a new location a few doors down. I never needed an appointment.

I finally got up the nerve to call with a request to dye my hair. "No problem," she informed me and said to come in later that evening. A late appointment was good in that I would probably be her last customer. No witnesses. Lynda dyed my hair, and boy was it dark!

My mother moved here in 1982 and lived in Riley View Apartments and, in her later years, was a resident of the Mennonite Memorial Home in Bluffton. I would visit her a few times each week and decided to pay her a visit after my dye job. I always valued her opinion and felt sure she would have something good to say about my new look. Mom was legally blind and couldn't hear. She could see well enough to get around and watch television, even though the figures on the TV were quite blurred, but she couldn't see well enough to read.

When I arrived she greeted me as usual, "Hi, Jeepie." She always called me Jeepie. Since childhood, everybody always called me Jeep; mom was the only one to add "ie." I guess it reminded her that I was still her "baby" (being an only child, I was her only baby).

Everybody in my home town of Nelsonville had a nickname. Frog, Soupy, Juke (my grandfather's), Popeye, Skillet, Shine (my dad's), Punk, Boulder, Tickey, Chicken Gravy, Woo Jimmy, Cash, etc. were a few of them. Each name had a story behind it, and mine was no exception. According to my mother, when I was a few days old, my cousin said that I looked like Jeep, a cartoon character in the comic section of the Sunday paper. He was handsome, intelligent, and everybody loved him.

My dad's story was different. At birth, I had big ears and they stuck out. He said I looked like a Jeep going down the road with both doors open, thus the moniker Jeep. I like my mom's story better. Thanks to plastic surgeon Dr. Elliott Saferin in Toledo, my ears no longer protrude and my dad's story no longer applies, at least not the sticking out part of it.

After mom's greeting, and because of her poor vision, I pulled up a chair close to her so she could have a good look at my hair. I kept turning my head from side-to-side in hopes that she would notice my hair and make a positive comment, like "Jeepie, your hair really looks nice. It makes you look so much younger."

No response concerning my hair. We visited for some time, and mom never mentioned my newly-dyed locks. Finally, I kissed her, excused myself, and as I was leaving, she said in a loud voice that any person with impaired hearing could hear on the second floor of the facility, "Jeepie, what did you do to your head? Your hair looks like dead grass!"

That was my last dye job.

A Letter from Mom

As a head football coach, I was often requested to speak publically. I always took my job seriously, but I was never too serious about myself. People who get wrapped up in themselves make a small package. Or, more simply put, self-centered individuals are boring as hell.

If I spoke at a clinic I would talk about football, but most of my speeches were at social gatherings—Lions Club, Rotary, etc.—so I only briefly touched on our football program in those venues. Wanting to show another side of me, I usually poked fun at myself and my hillbilly background. I composed a bogus letter my mother had supposedly sent, and I would read it as part of my presentation. Some of the material in the letter I collected over the years from other sources, and some I fabricated. I would read the letter as if mom were reading it to me in an accent characteristic of a true hillbilly. The letter:

Dear Jeepie:

I'm writing this letter slow 'cause I know you can't read too fast.

We don't live where we did when you left. Your dad read in the paper that most accidents happen within twenty miles from home, so we moved.

Not to worry, dad took the house numbers with us so we don't have to change our address.

This new place has a washing machine. The first day I put three shirts in it, pulled the chain, and I haven't seen them since.

It only rained twice this week, three days the first time and four days the second time.

Your cousin Joe Bob was put back to the eighth grade for the third time. His mom thought he was doing OK in the ninth until he told the teacher that alphabet soup don't make no sense. The good news: although his teacher thinks he is smart, she is pretty sure he leveled off when he was about two.

About your sister, she had a baby this morning. Haven't found out if it is a boy or girl, so don't know if you are an aunt or uncle.

Your dad is working weekends as a bouncer at the First and Last Chance Saloon. He searches the people going in to see if they have a weapon on them. If they don't, he gives them one.

The funeral home called and said if we don't pay the final bill on grandma's funeral, up she comes.

Remember the coat you wanted me to send you? Aunt Sue said it would be a little too heavy to send in the mail with them heavy buttons, so I cut them off and put them in the pockets.

Someone dropped an old tomcat off at our back door. Grandpa thought he acted a little sluggish, so he took him to the vet. The vet force-fed him a whole bottle of castor oil (the tomcat, not grandpa). The last time we saw old Tom, he was ten miles south of town with three cats with him. One was digging, one was covering up, and one was scouting for new territory. They were moving pretty fast.

Dad put new carpet in our toilet. I liked it so well I had him run it all the way up to the house.

Emma has finished her piano lessons and is playing in the church. She is not too happy, in that the preacher wants to buy a new chandelier and she isn't sure if she can play it. Like Emma, I don't think we should spend all that money on a new chandelier that she may not be able to play, especially since we are in such bad need of lights in this church.

Alcohol finally got the best of Uncle Cecile, but he died happy. He was at a hog roast and fell into the whiskey vat. Ten men tried to save him, but he fought them off and finally drowned. We had him cremated and his body burned for three days.

Three of your friends went off the bridge in a pickup truck. One of them was driving and two were in the back. The driver got out. He rolled down the window and swam to safety. The other two drowned. They couldn't get the tailgate down.

A big business moved into town today, a 300-pound Avon lady.

Not much news this time. Nothing much happened. If you don't get this letter, let me know and I will write you another one. Don't call us, we'll call.

Love,
Mom
XOXO

P.S. Your school bought a new mule to use in driver's education and sex ed.

P.P.S. Quigley got out of prison and says, "Howdy."

Occasionally, mom would be in the audience and had to answer questions related to the letter. She always responded, "Jeepie is a bigger prevaricator than his dad!" I considered that as a compliment.

Mom was a teacher and taught in the Nelsonville-York School System for 35 years. She spent the last years of her career as principal of Poston Elementary School (Kimberly, OH).

Mom died on April 25, 2009, at 11:10 p.m. I was at her bedside when she passed. She was 98. I still miss her counsel.

Letters from Home

Most players' parents were a delight, but some were a pain in the you-know-what. While at Bluffton, I received several hundred letters. Most were congratulatory or supportive, but some blasted me for not giving their son enough playing time. In my 35 years of college coaching, I never received an acrid letter from a parent whose son played a considerable amount of time.

A common complaint was, "You promised our son he would start." Never in my 35 years of college coaching have I ever promised a recruit he would start, except one. When I was at Ohio University, I recruited Archie Griffin, two-time Heisman winner at Ohio State. I promised Archie and his parents that he would start his freshman year. He is the only one to whom I made that promise. To this day, I stand by it.

Although I did tell every recruit and his parents that there was a chance of starting as a freshman, never did I tell any recruit he would be a starter at any time during his stay at Bluffton. I always stressed, "Whether you ever play a down, your most important accomplishment at Bluffton is to graduate." Some parents felt that their son's football accomplishments were more important than his education. Too bad!

I received three or four anonymous letters per year, always in complaint about something. Seldom would a complaining parent send a letter over his or her name. I have included an anonymous letter from a disgruntled parent. It is a bit lengthy, as most were, but it will give one an idea of how some parents reacted to their son not playing as much as they felt he should, even after a team victory. The entire, original letter, including the bold print, is that of the correspondent.

*From: Beavers Number 1 **DISAPPOINTED** Fan!!!!*
To: Carlin Carpenter

   *As the Beavers Number One Football fan I just wanted to take a moment to tell you how disappointed I am with Saturday's game. Yes we did win, but at what cost to your players? You have a large number of second-string upperclassmen football players that have put their heart and souls into your program and for what? You were up by three touchdowns, yet you still didn't put in the second string players. Why? Afraid that you might lose? I can understand not putting them in if you were only up by one touchdown, but you were up three. Do you really have that little of faith in your own team and your own program to give them a chance to play? I would bet that the majority of them were led to believe during recruiting that they would have a good chance to start…but when they get here there are already juniors and seniors in their positions so they act as tackling dummies in practice hoping that next year they will start. Well here it is their junior or senior year and they aren't playing! When up by three touchdowns as in to-day's case **upperclassmen should be given the opportunity to play most of the fourth quarter…especially when it is Parent's day!***

   I can understand that you feel they are not the best players but that is your fault because the players have never been given the opportunity to show what they are made of. You judge their ability on what you see in the JV games but this is not a true representation. They spend all practices running scout teams and never have a chance to practice as a JV team. They have had little or no actual practice…they are only tackling dummies to you…no wonder you have no faith in their ability.

What makes Saturday's game even worse is that was Parent's Day. By not putting in the second string players (senior or otherwise) you are basically telling the parents "your son is nothing more than a tackling dummy." **These players put their blood, sweat, and tears into your program and walk away with nothing!** *Every player that sat the bench on Saturday's game was slapped in the face by each and every one of you. Maybe it is time that you start realizing that there is more to winning and losing. What happened to the love of the game? The pride that players feel when they strap on their pads? The respect they receive for a good game?* **It is all gone!**

Not to be a pessimist but Bluffton has no shot at the play-offs…so **Saturday's game was NOT that important!** *The coaching staff, especially those calling the offensive plays, needs to grow some balls and stop running conservative plays! The defensive coordinator needs to teach the backs how to cover their receivers better. There were several instances in which a back could have intercepted the ball if he would have been paying attention.*

I have noticed that there are several positions in which freshmen are starting. Is this because they truly are better or because you are more concerned with the future success? I see how it is, "Get them in as freshman…gives them experience so that when they are seniors you will have a winning team again in four years." Carpenter, do you really want to wait four years before you become a successful coach again?

I realize that writing this letter has probably been a waste of time because I realize that A) most of you probably didn't even finish reading this letter, B) you won't change anything about the program, and C) you will still be too afraid of los-

ing to boost the self-esteem of your underclass and upperclass players by letting them play in the last game of the season for more than 2 minutes (anything less than 5 minutes is a slap in the face).

Thank you for taking the time to read this letter. I hope that when you bring this letter up in the nightly coaches meeting that you will find a way to make right with the second string players...because if you don't I guarantee that some of them will transfer at the end of the semester or the year just like Donnie Waddington and Mike Dane (the QB that beat you last week at Mount St. Joe did).

Truly Yours,
Beavers Number 1 DISAPPOINTED fan!!!!!

Whew! It was a small measure of comfort to read that, in addition to me, he or she also gave my offensive and defensive coordinators hell.

What this parent didn't know is that we had a junior varsity game scheduled for Monday, and if I had played the second team, they would not have been permitted to participate in Monday's game, as per NCAA rules. Had I violated this rule, it would result in their son's loss of eligibility. If Mr. or Ms. Number 1 DISAPPOINTED Fan's letter had not been anonymous, I could have explained the situation to him or her.

Obviously, I couldn't respond to anonymous letters, but most times responded to signed, derogatory ones to explain my position, unless it was in complaint of something ridiculous, such as, "Why didn't you shake my son's hand when you presented his award at the awards banquet?" I didn't waste my time on those.

I would often receive letters from players. As a matter of fact, I received one yesterday, March 31, 2012, from a player who was on the team I last coached. It follows:

Coach Carpenter:

Dan Rather once said, "The dream begins with a teacher who believes in you, who tugs and pushes and leads you to the next plateau, sometimes poking you with a sharp stick called "truth." I was recently named the 2012 National Football Foundation Assistant Coach of the Year by the Northeastern Ohio Chapter. When I thought back about all the great coaches that I've been blessed with in my life, your name and your coaching came to mind, and I wanted to take a minute to thank you for that. I truly believe without the great coaching that you provided to me at a critical stage of my life that such an award would have been beyond my reach.

When I arrived at Bluffton for my first visit, I'll never forget the personal tour that you gave to my mother and me. I remember asking you about the ring on your hand and you explained that the team had won it the previous year and that you planned on starting a collection. Even though that dream didn't come to fruition, I believe that I was very lucky to be on the last two teams that you coached and to have played football for you. You taught me many life lessons, Coach, while staying focused on trying to build successful football teams. I remember reporting to camp my sophomore year and being directed to your office where you moved me to guard. As a former tight end, not getting the ball didn't sound like a ton of fun to me. It pushed me to realize that football is an unselfish game and that on the offensive line you are truly a team player. Your work leads to the personal accomplishments of others, and in life there are no statistics. You are who you help and who you touch in your work, that is the most important lesson ever taught me, that is who you are.

While I can never fully repay you for all that you taught me and gave to me, what I can say is that this award is as much for you as it is for me. Without your guidance and pas-

sion I would not have turned out to be the coach that I am today. Every day that I walk out to practice, a workout, or a game I take a piece of your coaching with me. I firmly believe that this is what has allowed me to be successful in this field.

So in closing, thank you for who you are, what you do, and who you have helped me become.

Sincerely,
Alan Estep
Associate Head Football Coach
Oberlin College and Conservatory

In 2002, Alan was a starting sophomore offensive guard on the last team I coached, and since then he has had a successful college coaching career. I am very proud of his accomplishments.

I never paid much attention to derogatory letters, anonymous or otherwise, and was always careful not to allow the complimentary ones to inflate my ego more than it presently is. Admittedly, I do enjoy complimentary letters better.

Coaching is a Family Affair

The phone rang, "Hello."

"This is Bruce."

"Hey, Bruce! How's it going?"

"Darryl Gard committed suicide"

"What!?"

Darryl, a graduate of Buchtel High School (Akron, OH) was always smiling. I could hardly comprehend what I had just heard.

After his freshman year, I was informed by one of my players, that Darryl was considering transferring to Akron University. I immediately made arrangements to meet him and his mother for dinner. He was receptive to the idea, and agreed. I mentioned the rumor of him transferring, but he didn't confirm or deny it.

A few days later, Sharon and I went to Akron. We picked-up Darryl and his mother, Christine Washington, at his grandparents' home and proceeded to Red Lobster for the best meal money could buy. As we drove to the restaurant, we made small talk, but transferring was never mentioned. We also enjoyed dinner without any word of him leaving the program.

About halfway back to his grandparents' residence, without provocation, he blurted, "I'm staying at Bluffton." His mother was elated!

I was happy too, but surprised, "When did you decide that?"

"About two days ago. I never told mom."

I couldn't resist, "Damn Darryl, had I known you made that decision two days ago, we would have eaten at McDonalds." I can still hear him laughing.

Darryl Gard was the fastest running back I have ever coached. He was selected as first team NAIA District 22 in 1989 and 1990. After graduation, he played professionally in Arena Football for several years, after which he became an ordained Baptist minister and was Associate Pastor at the Livingstone Baptist Church, Akron.

He is survived by his wife, Deatra, and two sons, DeRon and Darius. I often think of Rev. Gard, number 33, and can still visualize him in repose, finally free from that hideous psychiatric disorder, depression.

Todd Alan Francis Hafner

Today, Thursday, April 26, 2012, I visited Todd at the Sujkowski Funeral Home in Toledo to pay my respects to his family. Todd passed away on Monday, April 23 from pancreatic cancer. Todd was a 1980 graduate of Toledo Central Catholic High School and graduated from Bluffton College in 1984.

Of all the players I have ever coached, he was the hardest worker. To improve his play, he reported to practice early and stayed late. He was totally dedicated to our program. He had dislocated his shoulder in high school wrestling and never had it properly repaired. Every couple of weeks, it would dislocate again, causing him gut-wrenching pain. Todd wouldn't wait for a trainer to reduce it; the nearest player would pull on his arm until his shoulder returned to its normal position. He would pop up ready for the next play. Not once in four years did he miss practice or a game.

While visiting with his parents, Robert and Arlene, at the funeral home, they told me why he came to Bluffton. When they started the story, I was sure it was because of my persistent calls, letters, and charismatic personality; however, my recruiting efforts had nothing to do with his commitment to BC. His father informed me that Todd chose Bluffton because there was a soft ice cream machine in our dining hall. I'm thankful for the machine and his propensity for the creamy delight it dispensed. He was a pleasure to coach. Whenever one needed a lift, all one had to do was talk to Todd. He bubbled with personality, and his laugh was catching.

Todd often phoned me with, "This is the best defensive lineman you ever coached!"

I would always respond, "No you weren't! You are the next best, but I can't remember his name."

Todd was first team NAIA District 22 in 1982 and 1983. He is survived by his wife of 22 years, Lorie, and three children, Audrie, Madilyn, and Lukas.

Early in my career, I attended former players' weddings. Now it is funerals. I prefer weddings.

Coaching is a Family Affair

In all of my 35 years of college coaching, I have had the unwavering support of my family. Sharon has stood by me in the good and bad times; from being fired, to almost being fired, to moving eighteen times, missing events in which our children participated, being away from home for extended times while recruiting, and tolerating my mood swings based on wins and losses. I could fill several pages with behavior that would drive any spouse to a lawyer.

I was married to football, but thankfully so was Sharon, as were our daughters, Kelly and Jill. One of the foremost reasons coaches leave the profession is the isolation that spouses sometimes experience, which either ends in divorce or coaches abandoning their careers. Sharon was always a part of what I was doing. She made home visits, met with parents and recruits when they visited campus, and never, ever missed a game, except when we played in Mexico.

After our children were born, they too attended every game. While Kelly and Jill were in high school, they worked on the sideline in some capacity. Both attended Bluffton College, and Kelly worked in the athletic department as a secretary. Jill was a member of our athletic training staff for the duration of her stay at BC.

When our granddaughter, Jill's Alexa, was five, she was ever present on our sideline in her "Beaver suit." Knowing they all were near always gave me a feeling of confidence. I wish our three other grandchildren had been born prior to my retirement. I'm sure that Jill's children, Carlin and Kaley, and Kelly's Bryce, would have enjoyed the pageantry and excitement of a football game in which grandpa was coaching. I know that I would have reveled having them in the stands.

An old man lives with his memories and a young man with his dreams. My dreams have been fulfilled and, thanks to my family, I have many treasured memories.

Epilogue

Over the years, I have had some great assistant coaches. Most knew more about the game than I, so I didn't have to do much. There were eight who had an accumulation of over 90 years on my staff—Greg Brooks, 23 years; Allen Curtiss, 15; Louie Stokes, 15; Denny Phillips, 14; Denny Shaner, 7; Ed Stults, 7; Herb Purton, 5; and Mike Richards, 5. Louie, both Dennys, Ed, Herb, and Mike taught in the public school system, and would come to practice immediately after class and remain until our staff meeting was adjourned at 10 p.m.—four nights per week. That's dedication!

Also, there were others who served, but for fewer years. All of my assistants were adjunct, except Greg and Allen, while employed at another job full-time. Although the assistant jobs were classified as part-time, they were anything but. Attending meetings, practices, and games required them to spend as many as six to eight hours per day, in addition to their regular employment. We had many intense arguments over philosophy, but always left the day as friends.

Denny Phillips was the slowest to anger, so if he got mad, I considered it a worthwhile argument. Louie and Denny Phillips are still coaching at the University. I owe all of them a debt of gratitude, as well as the wonderful women in their lives; Carol, Phyllis, Melanie, Kaye, Susan, Pam, Connie, and Jane which I can never repay.

Phill Talavinia, our athletic trainer, and I worked together for eighteen years. His dedication to our program and the long hours he endured are very much appreciated. When the coaches' day was done, his began. If he were paid an hourly wage for the time he spent preventing and treating injuries, Phill could have retired ten years ago. The only criticism I have of Phill is that he drives too fast and tailgates. On the positive side, when I ride with him, his driving always brings me closer to Jesus. Phill now serves as the director of athletics. His wife, Michelle, endures the long hours he is away from home while performing the duties of an athletic administrator.

For those several hundred players who have donned a Beaver uniform, and support personnel who have worked on the sideline, thank you for your contribution to the great game of football, and especially, Bluffton's program. I appreciate your involvement and wish you the best.

When I arrived in Bluffton, I had planned to leave as soon as I could secure a position at a Division I institution. Once I realized what an ideal situation this was, I had to stay. Never in my career have I worked with so many wonderful people. The extraordinary talents of our faculty and staff defy description, and their dedication to their professions is beyond reproach. I can never repay them for what they have done for Sharon, Kelly, Jill, and me. They are the GREATEST! From this ole' hillbilly to all of my fellow Beavers, I extend a heartfelt thank you for your support and the kaleidoscope of memories.

Bluffton Football: 1979-2002

Players, Coaches, Trainers, Managers, Cheerleaders, and Support Personnel

Adams, Chad
Agler, Pat
Akers, Don
Akers, Mike
Akers, Robin
Alexander, Jim
Alexander, Ryan
Allen, Derek
Allmon, Seve
Allshouse, Jennifer
Altman, David
Amstutz, Jane
Anderson, Bart
Anderson, Cary
Anderson, Cory
Anderson, Jason
Andews, Jason

Ansley, Greg
Anter, Tami
Apple, Dawn
Apt, Stacie
Arend, Jeremy
Armstrong, Andy
Arp, Mindy
Arps, Janeen
Arrasmith, Doug
Asher, Brian
Atkinson, Chris
Augustyniak, Scott
Aura, Mike
Austin, Elton
Bachelor, Cory
Baemel, Christine
Bagenstose, James

Bailey, Rob
Baker, Jenny
Baker, Vince
Bame, Bob
Barber, Gabriel
Barber, Kim
Barberree, Bill
Barman, Jeff
Barnes, Dave
Barnhill, Dave
Barr, Jim
Bartsch, Jon
Basinger, Jessica
Basinger, Tom
Baskerville, Randy
Bassett, Josh
Batchelor, Eric

Batey, Dennis
Bauer, Don
Bauer, Ron
Bauman, Suzy
Bauman, Ted
Baumer, Troy
Baumgartner, Keith
Beachum, Cardell
Beachy, Andy
Beard, Richard
Beavers, Scott
Bechtel, Shawn
Beck, Lori
Beeker, Brent
Beer, David
Beidelschies, Beau
Beitle, Sara
Benefit, Jaime
Benner, John
Benroth, Jim
Benroth, Mike
Benton, Dan
Bernath, Chuck
Bernath, Jeff
Bertsche, Brian
Bihn, Chris
Bishop, Noell
Bissell, George
Black, DeAnn
Black, Don
Black, Joshua
Blair, Craig
Blair, Deb

Blair, OJ
Blankenship, Kenny
Blevins, Shaun
Blose, Wendy
Bodi, Michael
Boenker, Tony
Boise, Perry
Bostater, Kim
Bowerman, Russell
Bowers, Nate
Bowers, Ryan
Bowling, Warner
Bowser, Dean
Bowsher, Adam
Boyd, Kolin
Brandeberry, Lisa
Brattoli, David
Bricker, Sherry
Brinker, Scott
Brisbois, Michael
Brooks, Greg
Browder, Joel
Brown, Jeff
Brown, Tim
Brubaker, Deb
Brubaker, Jay
Brucker, Dave
Brueggemeir, Amy
Brunell, Mollie
Bruns, Greg
Buck, Jacob
Bultrowicz, Scott
Bump, Jeffrey

Burgess, Adam
Burkhart, Dave
Burkholder, Jill
Burkholder, Kevin
Burns, Michael
Burrey, Kim
Burroughs, Herb
Buscher, Todd
Buschur, Brent
Butler, Brian
Byers, Gerald
Byrkett, Troy
Cairns, Marshall
Callahan, Randy
Calver, Kevin
Campbell, Angie
Campbell, Granvile
Carder, Randy
Carmack, Jeff
Carmack, Scott
Carman, Rob
Carnes, Jeremy
Carnevale, Alan
Carney, Jack
Carpenter, Greg
Carpenter, Jill
Carpenter, Kelly
Carrion, Eric
Cash, Demond
Castle, Tony
Caton. Becky
Caudill, Ryan
Caulfield, Matt

Caven, Brett
Cavender, Chad
Chambers, Dan
Chambers, Todd
Chapman, Jeremy
Chase, David
Cheatwood, Melinda
Cheek, Craig
Cherry, Blaine
Chiles, Matt
Chinchar, Mike
Christensen, Chris
Cisco, Mark
Clark, Jeff
Clemens, Chris
Clemens, Matthew
Clemens, Nate
Clingman, Jim
Clouse, Greg
Clune, Mike
Cockerell, Mae
Colatruglio, Brian
Colatruglio, Nate
Colburn, Todd
Coleman, Ed
Coleman, John
Coleman, Pat
Collier, Everett
Collins, Bill
Collins, Lowell
Collum, Jeff
Combs, Byron
Company, Jeff

Conkel, James
Conkel, Steve
Contat, Brad
Cook, Dennis
Cook, Doug
Cook, Kevin
Cook, Zackariah
Coon, Carrie
Cooper, Matt
Cornele, Rick
Cornell, Brandie
Cornell, Tony
Cotterman, John
Cousino, Luke
Cowen, Neil
Cox, Marcus
Cox, Rob
Cozad, Jason
Cradcolph, Toussaint
Cramer, Mike
Crandall, Caleb
Crane, Drew
Craun, Patrick
Crawford, Ryan
Creque, Mark
Criblez, Lance
Cripe, Craig
Cross, Steve
Crutchfield, Brian
Culver, Del
Cunningham, Jeffrey
Cupples, Brandon
Curtis, Josh

Curtis, Lee
Curtis, Mark
Curtiss, Allen
Cutnaw, Kyle
Cutright, Ryan
Dales, Chris
Damewood, Brian
Dane, Mike
Daniel, Matt
Daniel, Sam
Darney, Matt
Daugherty, Dale
Davasko, Missy
Davis, Jerry
Davis, Mike
Dawes, Bob
Debo, Duane
Degler, Chic
DeHaven, John
Delsmith, Kathryn
Denning, Pat
Dennis, Bill
Dennis, Scott
Detwiler, Jon
Detwiler, Kim
DeWitt, Matt
Dickey, Terry
Dieringer, Joe
Diller, Andy
Diller, Sarah
Dion, Greg
Ditz, Greg
Dobson, Steve

Dodds, Ben

Doner, Jackie

Donohue, Derek

Doty, Cheryl

Douglass, Robert

Drake, Elaine

Dryfuse, Jim

Dubois, Tim

Duerk. Scott

Duff, Scott

Dunbrack, Jennifer

Durrah, Steve

Dwenger, Jim

Earl, Dianne

Earley, Duane

Ebersbach, Dave

Echols, Roosevelt

Eddy, William

Edgington, Tony

Edinger, Joe

Edinger, John

Edwards, Beth

Ehrman, Jim

Eichert, Jason

Elkins, Reginald

Ellis, Dion

Elson, Derrick

Elwood, Norman

Ely, Matt

Engel, Ken

Engle, Steve

Englehardt, D J

Epp, Ronald

Ernst, Kim

Ervin, Audrey

Estep, Alan

Etter, Thonda

Etts, Jim

Etzler, Chris

Evans, Ken

Evans, Nick

Fabrizio, Dominic

Fader, Tosha

Fairchild, Chad

Fairchild, Lon

Fairchild, Shane

Falb, Ron

Falloon, Chris

Farlow, Rocky

Faulk, Barak

Fay, Jeff

Featherstun, Lonie

Ferenbaugh, Connie

Ferrell, Joe

Ferrell, Randy

Fessler, Scott

Finerd, C J

Finnen, Leah

Fisher, Bill

Fisher, Chris

Fisher, Mark

Fisher, Matt

Fisher, Ron

Fist, Sherry

Flathers, Scott

Fleming, Jerry

Flick, Bob

Flowers, Ross

Fogt, Eric

Fortkamp, Jeff

Fortman, John

Fortman, Nikki

Fortman, Tony

Foster, Corey

Fox, Clint

Fox, Darrin

Fox, James

Frank, Glenn

Frazee, George

Frederick, Kristen

Freeman, Ray

Fritz, Jeremiah

Frizzell, Korey

Fry, Jeffrey

Fryman, Dustin

Fulton, Derrick

Furnas, Kevin

Gabes, Shaun

Gable, Bill

Gable, Carl

Gable, Mark

Gainous, Ron

Galzerano, John

Gansheimer, Rich

Gard, Darryl

Gardner, Bruce

Garee, Robert

Garza, Yolanda

Gates, Darrin

Gehman, Diane
Geiser, Jon
Geiser, Ron
Genslinger, Kile
George, Curtis
Gephart, Brian
Gerber, Shawn
Gerding, Steve
Gerschutz, Lonnie
Geuy, Jon
Giesige, Steve
Giesken, Mike
Giesken, Tom
Gilanyi, Roger
Gilcrease, Greg
Gilger, Pat
Gingrich, Mel
Gladwell, Stacy
Glick-Colquett, Karen
Glista, Rich
Glore, Dave
Godfrey, Anthony
Goedde, Mike
Goetz, Shawn
Gogci, Jon
Goings, Tyson
Goldfuss, Cory
Good, Craig
Gorsuch, Dianne
Govito, Pete
Graham, Patrick
Grant, John
Gratz, Lori

Green, Justin
Greene, Zack
Gremling, Mark
Grieser, Lisa
Grieshop, Dixie
Griffith, Carlton
Grote Mike
Groves, Abraham
Groves, Jason
Gump, Kevin
Guncy, Brian
Gussler, Nick
Gwirtz, Amy
Habegger, Arman
Habegger, Luke
Hadley, Mike
Hafner, Todd
Hager Mike
Hale, Greg
Hale, Nate
Hall, Bobby
Haman, Steve
Hamilton, Matt
Hamman, Chad
Hamman, Doug
Hammond, Chris
Hancock, Pat
Hand, Mike
Hanes Chad
Hanes Todd
Harden, James
Harding, John
Harmon, Jalene

Harms, Chris
Harrington, Casey
Harris, Danny
Harris, Fred
Harris, Jeff
Harris, Mike
Harrod, Bill
Hart, Randy
Hatcher, Todd
Hathaway, Scott
Hauenstein, Charles
Hauenstein, Neil
Haughawout, Tim
Haumesser, Donna
Hawkins, Chris
Hayden, Rob
Heatherly, Jim
Heatwole, Kelly
Heckman, Troy
Hedleston, Tim
Hedrick, Mark
Hefner, James
Heinz, Brian
Hellyer, Chet
Hemmert, Cliff
Henderson, Dawn
Henderson, Ethan
Henderson, Stan
Henline, Jason
Henry, Steve
Herman, Julie
Herr, Mardy
Herrick, Tanya

Hershey, Terry

Hershiser, Jeff

Hertzfeld, Shawn

Hertzfeld, Tara

Hidey, John

Hight, Dan

Hill, Julie

Hill, Yohana

Hilt, William

Hilty, Tom

Hobbs, Jasper

Hoffinger, Brian

Hoffman, Leslie

Hofstetter, Jeanette

Hoge, Alan

Holbrook, Scott

Holdegreve, Chrissy

Holder, Mike

Holfinger, Brian

Hollenbach, Chip

Hollowell, Robert

Holtz, Craig

Holzwart, John

Hood, Heath

Horn, Travis

Horner, Chuck

Hosack, Jeffrey

Hostetler, Bryce

Hostetler, George

Houston, David

Howard, Tim

Hoye, Joe

Hubbard, Kip

Hubbard, Sylvester

Huber, Chris

Huber, Darrell

Huber, Larry

Hucke, Dave

Hucke, Dennis

Hughes, Kenny

Hughes, Mark

Hughett, Leisel

Hull, Travis

Humphrey, Dick

Hunsinger, Eric

Hunter, Dennis

Hunter, Ty

Hupp, Kurt

Hurd, John

Hurford, William

Hurt, Thomas

Huston, Ron

Hutchison, Jon

Hutchinson, Mike

Iocovetta, Chad

Irons, Christopher

Jackson, Bob

Jackson, Greg

Jackson, Jason

Jackson, John

Jackson, Michael

Jackson, Patti

Jackson, Ron

Jacobs, Matt

Jacoby, Eliza

James. Kenny

Jankovich, Steve

Jefferson, James

Jenkins, Neil

Johnson, Geald

Johnson, Jovan

Johnson, Paul

Johnson, Randy

Jones, Audwin

Jones, Clay

Jones, James

Jones, Molly

Joyce, Glen

Jurrus, Max

Karalia, Simone

Karamol, Dan

Katzler, Robert

Keating, Kerry

Keaton, Gene

Keegan, Erika

Kehres, Mary

Keim, Brian

Keith, Nathan

Kellermeyer, Lance

Kelly, Brian

Kelly, Mike

Kemp, LauraLee

Kempf, Diane

Kendrick, Perry

Kern, Becky

Kessler, Laura

Ketner, Chris

Ketterman, Paul

Kieninger, Steve

Kille, Tonya
Kimmet, John
Kin, Tobi
King, Allan
King, Bob
King, Herb
King, Jamie
King, John
King, Kristi
King, Matt
King, Monica
King, Phillip
Kinn, Jon
Kinn, Larry
Kintner, Bill
Kirkton, Jonathon
Kirkton, Todd
Kisor, Doug
Kissinger, Lowell
Kitchen, Rob
Kleininger, Steve
Kline, Nate
Knepper, Sharon
Knight, Kris
Knisley, Heath
Knodel, JJ
Knoop, Scott
Koepfier, Jim
Koerner, Teresa
Koontz, Ken
Koontz, Tim
Krabill, Bill
Kracium, Dan

Kraft, Josh
Kreider, Nathan
Kreigh, Eric
Krieger, Aaron
Kroeger, Jon
Krupp, Julie
Kruse, Tim
Kucera, Steve
Kyle, Jeff
LaCroix, Keith
Laffin, Brian
LaGrange, Scott
Lahmer, Ian
Laipply, Wes
Lamb, Jennifer
Lane, Dale
Lange, Allison
LaVeck, Dave
Lawhorn, Kevin
Lawless, Kerry
Lawrence, Adam
Lawwell, Scott
Leeper, Jodi
Leeper, Terri
Leeth, Eric
Leffler, Ray
Lehman, Alicia
Lehman, Jason
Lehman, Jeff
Lehman, Keaton
Lehman, Lance
Lehman, Paula
Leimeister, Mike

Lentz, Kyle
Leonard, Dick
Lepley, Travis
Leslie, Jenny
Leuthold, Sean
Lewis, Greg
Lewis, Jason
Leyda, Jamie
Lias, Kevin
Lindloff, Bryan
Link, Jerry
Lintner, Carrie
Lippincott, David
List, Kevin
Lockmiller, Steve
Lodwick, Rick
Loeb, Cindy
Logan, Rick
Long, Shawn
Longstreath, Mike
Lorenzen, Robert
Lovell, Trent
Lowther, Mike
Luginbill, Douglas
Luginbuhl, Roger
Luttfiing, Rich
Lutz, Doug
Lutz, Doug
Lybarger, Mike
Lyman, Ryan
Lyon, Anne
Macey, Branden
Mackey, Chris

Mager, Scott

Mahas, Ben

Maize, Bill

Major, Jeff

Malone, Roger

Malone, Tim

Mangrum, Mac

Mankin, Wendie

Manns, Roger

Mapes, Scott

Marchetti, Nick

Markley, Sharon

Marquart, Doug

Marshall, Kurt

Marshall, Tom

Martinez, Chuck

Mason, Bob

Mason, Damian

Mason, Tina

Massie, Stephanie

Matthews, Zachary

Maxey, Wayne

Maynard, Ted

McAfee, Dale

McBride, Dwight

McCammon, Tevis

McCann, Jeff

McCauley, Joe

McClain, Nathan

McClain, Rioroan

McClendon, Eddie

McClure, Shelly

McClure, Terry

McConnell, Pete

McCormick, Pat

McCoy, David

McCraney, Tim

McDaniel, Tom

McDonald, Dan

McDonald, Dr. Mark

McDonough, Chris

McDowell, Milt

McDowell, Elizabeth

McGlaughlin, Sean

McGue, Pat

McInturf, Jan

McKean, Craig

McKinney, Paul

McLaughlin, Pat

McMillen, David

McMillon, Darryl

McNeal, Larry

McNett, Mike

McPeek, Robert

McQuown, Eric

McRae, Jason

McSweeney, Larry

McVicar, David

Mendiola, Bennie

Mercy, Jeff

Mershman, Jonathan

Mesker, Ron

Messman, April

Metz, Eric

Metzger, Allen

Michael, Joseph

Mick, Joel

Mickens, Shawn

Middleton, Stewart

Miller, Ben

Miller, Eric

Miller, Kelly

Miller, Leon

Miller, Margie

Miller, Rich

Mills, Amanda

Mills, Wayne

Minnifield, Greg

Minnig, Scott

Minto, Bob

Mintz, Corey

Miree, David

Mirones, Anthony

Mitchell, Matt

Modd, Andy

Mohr, Jan

Montgomery, Doug

Montgomery, Jesse

Moon, Jerry

Moore, Brad

Moore, Jacob

Moore, Rachel

Moore, Randy

Moosey, Chip

Morehead, Ricky

Morgan, Kevin

Morris, Courtnee

Morris, Michael

Mort, Tony

Morton, Rashid
Moser, Chris
Moser, Kim
Mosteller, Randy
Mowery, Ward
Moyer, Dave
Moyer, Phil
Mull, Charles
Mullins, Donald
Murphy, Pat
Myatt, Michael
Myers, Corby
Myers, John
Myers, Mark
Nafziger, Pete
Naumann, Tami
Neiswander, Andi
Nester, Darryl
Neuenschwander, Kevin
Nevergall, Brent
Nichols, Steven
Nicol, Brian
Nicol, Tom
Nightingale, Kurt
Nisly, Keith
Nofziger, Vance
Nolan, Andy
Nolin, Brandon
Norris, Bill
Norris, Charles
Norris, Les
Norwood, Omar
Nowak, John

Nowlin, Andy
Numbers, Josh
Nussbaum, Eric
Nyler, Tim
O'Brien, James
Obencur, Keith
Odenweller, Trish
Oehlers, Andrew
Ogle, Trevor
Oliver, Craig
Orr, Rick
Osborn, Jon
Osborn, Scott
Osterland, Ben
Ostermeier, Gary
Ott, Tony
Overmyer, Timothy
Owen, Steve
Owens, Jared
Pahl, Staci
Pallay, Gib
Palmer, Robert
Pannabecker, Tim
Pappas, Chris
Paprocki, Mike
Parete, Suzanne
Parker, Tom
Parkins, John
Parlette, Vicki
Parrett, Joel
Parsons, Scott
Parthemore, Jeremy
Paulus, Dan

Paver, Steve
Paxton, Ed
Perkins, David
Perkins, Robert
Perko, Melissa
Peters, Shawn
Peterson, Gerald
Pettus, Zac
Petty, Becki
Petty, Bobbi
Phillips, Denny
Phillips, Sean
Phillips, Todd
Philpot, T J
Piansek, Robert
Pierce, Dan
Pittenger, Kim
Pitzer, Stephanie
Plymale, Lee
Poeppelman, Jeremy
Poling, Jim
Poplar, Kristen
Portik, Jim
Portis, David
Porzelius, Kris
Powall, Michael
Powell, Bart
Powell, Nick
Pratt, Missy
Pressley, Orlando
Price, Keith
Prichard, Randy
Pruitt, Aric

Puckett, Kelli

Pullen, Mark

Pursel, Matt

Purton, Herb

Pyle, Roger

Qualls, Dan

Rabley, Brad

Ragan, Mike

Raglow, Bob

Ramage, Rob

Ramsey, Cornelius

Ramsey, Sara

Rasnic, Dan

Rausch, Rich

Ray, Michelle

Rayner, Rod

Reed, Eugene

Reeder, Ricky

Reichard, Gary

Reichenbach, Neil

Reichenbach, Todd

Renshaw, Lamarr

Reyes, Domenic

Rhoads, Jason

Richards, Mike

Richardson, Jonathan

Richardson, Steve

Richeson, Kevin

Ridgeway, Janeen

Riggenbach, Brett

Risley, Steve

Risner, Paul

Ritter, Shawn

Roach, Steve

Robbins, Mark

Robinson, Brian

Robinson, Mark

Rodabaugh, Franklin

Rodabaugh, Fred

Roethlisberger, Ben

Rogers, John

Rogers, Wyndell

Roll, Zach

Roper, Chip

Rosich, Rick

Ross, David

Ross, Kevin

Ross, Lisa

Ross, Rick

Rossman, Donnie

Round, Travis

Ruckman, James

Ruffin, Rashawn

Runneals, Mike

Rush, Stephanie

Russell, Jim

Ruthenberg, Casey

Sabus, Mike

Salyers, Nick

Sammons, Bill

Sammons, John

Samsal, David

Sandberg, Hugo

Satchell, Chris

Saum, Lon

Saurer, Jason

Savage, Heath

Schantz, Susan

Schantz, Tom

Schelb, Kevin

Schertz, Steve

Schiffel, Scott

Schill, Joseph

Schilling, Chris

Schinaman, Pete

Schindler, Scott

Schira, Doug

Schleter, David

Schlosser, Scott

Schmersal, Joanna

Schmersal, Rachel

Schmidt, Brian

Schneck, Barry

Schneider, Geofff

Scholz, Matt

Schotsch, Michael

Schott, Ian

Schroeder, Tyler

Schultz, Dianna

Schultz, Michael

Schumacher, Jennifer

Schumacher, Liz

Schwab, Ben

Schwab, Brad

Scribner, Chuck

Seibert, Tanisha

Selbee, Brad

Sellers, Kelly

Sells, Ethan

Semelsberger, Tim
Sesslar, Marcus
Severns, Jack
Shackleford, Nichole
Shafer, Avril
Shafer, Chip
Shaffer, Kim
Shaner, Denny
Shaner, Jeff
Shannon, John
Shatto, Jason
Shedd, Todd
Sheely, David
Shell, Jarrett
Shetler, Luther
Shilling, Chris
Shingler, John
Shipp, Luke
Shivley, Dan
Shobe, Jeremy
Shoemaker, Bill
Shofner, Casey
Shoope, Reid
Shoope, Ryan
Short, Andy
Short, Lacey
Short, Michelle
Short, Steve
Short, Sue
Shoupe, Aaron
Shoupe, Stephen
Shreiner, Tim
Shumaker, Scott

Simcox, Eric
Simms, Thomas
Simpkins, Zach
Sindelar, Mike
Sindelar, Scott
Singer, Brian
Skaggs, Leslie
Slaughter, Josh
Slough, Ken
Smiddy, Gary
Smiddy, Jamie
Smiddy, Shannon
Smith, Daniel
Smith, Duane
Smith, Gary
Smith, Jason
Smith, Kevin
Smith, Larry
Smith, Ricardo
Smith, Toby
Smith, Tom
Smith, Tony
Smotrila, Jarrett
Snyder, Gregg
Snyder, Molly
Soloman, Matthew
Solomon, Steve
Somers, Amber
Sommer, Christine
Sommer, Mark
Sommers, Chris
Sommers, Stacy
Sonneberger, Carl

Sopkovich, Eric
Sorrell, Aaron
Sorrell, Luke
Souder, Jere
South, Audra
Spagnola, Leo
Spain, Mary
Spallinger, Amy
Sparks, Kevin
Spath, Mike
Speicher, Susan
Spence, Bryce
Sperk, Ryan
Spicer, Kevin
Spisak, Chris
Spradling, Jonathon
Spragg, Van
Sprow, Cory
Staats, Steve
Stacey, Chris
Stacy, Scott
Stafford, Tim
Staples, Tyrell
Steiner, Brian
Steiner, Jesse
Steiner, Mary
Steiner, Scott
Steiner, Steve
Steinmetz, Mark
Stenson, Deb
Sterk, Marcel
Stettler, Barbara
Stevens, James

Stevens, Bruce

Stevens, Marty

Stevens, Mike

Stewart, Spencer

Stewart, Tiffany

Stockton, Jeff

Stokes, Louis

Stokes, Micheline

Stoller, Aaron

Stolly, Logan

Stoops, Arthur

Stopher, Bret

Stork, Nicholas

Stoughton, Lanny

Strable, Laura

Strahley, Kevin

Stratton, Steve

Strayer, Kerry

Stried, Tim

Striker, Jerome

Strock, Tory

Stroker, Jim

Stubbins, Lee

Stults, David

Stults, Ed

Subler, Kevin

Suchy, Ronald

Sullivan, Chuck

Sunderhaus, Greg

Sunderhaus, Mike

Suter, Tim

Suter, Tom

Sutherin, Andrew

Swanson, Matt

Swyers, Bill

Szakacs, Steve

Taber, Ryan

Tabler, Amy

Tabler, Andy

Tabler, Jim

Tabler, Joe

Tabler, John

Tackett, Josh

Talavinia, Phill

Taray, Mike

Tate, Bill

Tatum, Vido

Taviano, Luke

Taylor, Greg

Taylor, Matt

Taylor, Michael

Teague, Mike

Teglovic, Ryan

Terhark, Trent

Thomas, Bryant

Thomas, Josh

Thomas, Ron

Thompson, Dave

Thompson, Gerry

Thompson, Tyree

Thornell, Nikki

Timmons, Jeff

Tobin, Rick

Tong, Tracey

Tougher, Michael

Traucht, Lucas

Treen, Carl

Treen, Chad

Trentine, Josh

Troyer, Deana

Tryon, Gail

Tryon, Tracy

Turley, Todd

Turner, Joe

Tussing, Adam

Tussing, Jason

Urwin, Laura

Van Eman, Scott

Van Eman, Stephanie

Van Hoose, Dana

VanAusdal, Matt

Vasko, Tony

Vaughn, Andy

Vergith, Lindsey

Vermillion, Jason

Vermillion, Josh

Vermillion, Steve

Viegas, Curtis

Vielma, David

Vincent, Jeff

Violand, Pat

Vogt, Jim

Voress, Daniel

Voress, Neal

Voss, Dennis

Waddington, Donny

Wade, Carlos

Wadley, Randy

Wagner, James

Wagner, Pat
Wainwright, Chris
Wakefield, Dan
Wakefield, Vince
Walker, Leif
Walker, Roshanee
Walker, Scott
Walter, Kris
Walters, Troy
Walton, Nate
Wangler, Matt
Wannamaker, Jim
Wanyerka, Mark
Warburg, Frank
Ward, Dave
Ward, Evan
Ward, Shelby
Warnyerka, Mark
Watkins, Domont
Watkins, John
Waugh, Reggie
Weaver, J Denny
Weaver, Michelle
Webb, Sheri
Webb, Toneli
Weber, Jeremy
Weese, Patrick

Weigandt, Jason
Weisenbarger, Phil
Welch, Chris
Welch, Traci
Wenger, Ed
West, Dan
Whitaker, Ryan
White, Randy
Whitley, Brent
Wier, Benjamin
Wierwille, Dave
Wiggins, Wayne
Wilcox, Aaron
Wild, Mike
Wilhelm, James
Wilkerson, Kevin
Williams, Aaron
Williams, Burt
Williams, Dan
Williams, Dennis
Williams, Mary
Williams, Jesse
Willis, Dani
Willoughby, Cliff
Wilson, Bernie
Wilson, Donald
Wilson, Lucas

Wilson, Michael
Winters, Sean
Wirick, David
Wiseman, Matt
Witmer, Mike
Wittmer, Amy
Wolfe, Donald
Wolfe, Jack
Wolpert, Karl
Woodard, Beth
Woods, Brian
Woods, Sarah
Woodson, Brad
Woolace, Evan
Wortman, Darryl
Wrasman, Kevin
Wright, Jason
Wulff, Jeff
Wyndham, Brienne
Yeager, Shelley
Yoder, Brooke
Young, Todd
Zeh, David
Zerger, Becky
Zickafoose, Jon
Zimmerman, Kevin
Zuver, Tony

Acknowledgments

André Swartley of Workplay Publishing served as my publisher. He is presently in Japan teaching English and took time from his busy schedule to assist me with the publication. His patience with me and diligent editing are very much appreciated. His students in Japan are fortunate to have such a competent teacher.

Mr. Fred Steiner, one of my editors, knows his business. I could not have written this book without his professional guidance. Thanks, Fred!

Grammar and spelling experts, Ron and Alice Lora, read the original manuscript and helped me conjugate some verbs, but didn't change "ain't" in the title, *Coaching Football Ain't Easy*, because it ain't. I am forever grateful for their assistance.

As well as editors, Don and Nancy Schweingruber were my censors. They examined my work for the purpose of suppressing parts deemed objectionable. If you were offended, blame them.

I would be remiss not to mention Tami Forbes, my boss. She is chairperson of our department and put up with me until my retirement in 2003. I have never known her to lose her temper, and Lord knows I have given her plenty of opportunities to do so.

I am thankful for the coaches and their wives; Bill and Katie Hess, Joe and Lil Dean, Frank and Pat Ellwood, Cliff and Elsa Heffelfinger, Bob and Jo Kappes, and Frank and Ruth Richey at Ohio University for taking a chance on a young, untested coach from Nelsonville. They will always occupy a special place in my memories.

A special tribute is in order for my parents, Jean and Shine, and my in-laws, Norma and Homer O'Nail. They never lost faith in me. Their love and support were unconditional. It wasn't until I saw their names chiseled in granite did I appreciate the magnitude of their presence.

About the Author

Former head football coach and director of athletics at Bluffton College, Carlin Carpenter retired from coaching in 2002 after winning a Bluffton College school record of 103 games. At the time of his retirement, he was the dean of active Ohio college head football coaches. Carpenter served Bluffton as head football coach for 24 years, and 23 as director of athletics. He is still employed by the university as Professor Emeritus and is a member of the teaching faculty.

After his arrival at Bluffton in 1979, Carpenter guided some of BC's most prolific teams. From 1985 through 1990, his teams fashioned a 44-13 record, and was nationally ranked each year. The Beavers competed in the 1987 and 1988 national playoffs. Three of his teams, 1985, 1987, and 1988, have been inducted into the Bluffton University Athletic Hall of Fame. Carpenter has been named conference or district coach of the year seven times. He is a member of the Athletic Hall of Fame at his alma mater, Defiance College, as well as the Athletic Hall of Fame at Bluffton University.

Carpenter served as chairman of the American Football Coaches Association Coach of the Year Committee for five years. Originally from Nelsonville, Ohio, he is an accomplished motivational speaker, storyteller, humorist, and guitarist. His many appearances have taken him to numerous venues including Dallas, New Orleans, and Nashville where he spoke and performed at the Grand Ole Opry Hotel.

A graduate of Defiance (OH) College with a degree in psychology and biology, Carpenter earned his master's degree at Ohio University. He has held coaching positions at Defiance College, Ohio University, and served as defensive coordinator at Marshall University. Carpenter is a U.S. Navy veteran.

Carpenter is married to Sharon O'Nail. Both are graduates of Nelsonville High School. They have two children, Kelly and Jill.